International Book Number: 0 948964 52 9

THE VOICE OF AT-HLAN

Channeled Information
from
Atlantis to Sirius

Roger Keenan © 1996

Published by Pyramid Publications
15 Nut Bush Lane · Torquay · TQ2 6SA · U.K.
in association with and produced by
Rotographic Publications
37 St. Efrides Road · Torquay · TQ2 5SG · U.K.

Acknowledgements

I am grateful for all those who sat in the White Feather Circle and later in the Circle of Ten at my home. Particular thanks are due to Patsy, Kerry-Anne, Hannah, Lenette, Teresa and Susan who, in a select circle, deepened the questioning and searched the universe. The book would not have been completed without the dedication and commitment of Patsy who, being a Psychic Artist, foresaw its completion, and my sister Ann, whose patience at the computer was beyond my understanding!

Finally my grateful appreciation is given to At-Hlan who started the process and never let us down.

To Audrey, with love.

The Voice of At-Hlan

The Voice of At-Hlan

Introduction

Many mediums, I suppose, meditate in various ways to become more sensitised and aware of the spiritual source that inspires them and enables them to become a channel or catalyst to link the world of the spirit and the present material world of earthly existence. With some, myself included, a rapport becomes established between self and spiritual guides and a visual and telepathic communication system ensues in which we all, as one, attempt to follow the same spiritual pathway.

Many people sit by themselves and/or in groups to send out thoughts for the well-being of the planet and for the spiritual awareness of all those souls that inhabit the world. For whatever colour, creed or culture we belong to we are all assuredly from some spiritual source - The Great Mind, God, The Primal Void or The Great White Spirit - the Father and Creator of all life.

Some years ago, when sitting quietly, I felt that a 'voice' was attempting to use my vocal chords to speak. After some guttural sounds were produced I had the impression that the 'being's' name Atlexa, who was from the fabled Atlantis and to produce the halting and guttural voice was, for some time, amusing but then forgotten as the pull and responsibilities of everyday life intruded.

About three years ago I had a heart attack with no enlightening or illuminating near-death experiences, just a lot of pain and a long convalescence. However, I was soon asked to join two home circles, the idea of which I rejected for some time, having got used to the strategy of sitting by myself and not wishing to 'sit in silence' with a lot of strangers. The offers were repeated several times and so I took myself to the first of the circles whose members were complete strangers to me. After a short time the 'voice' that I had heard several years previously seemed to be powerfully determined to be heard but, in the event of feeling foolish and embarrassed, I fought against it until my whole body shook. I then relaxed somewhat to hear (in a light trance) "I am At-Hlan, Warrior Priest of Atlantis and bring you greetings from the world of Spirit", and the voice continued to answer questions, of a simple nature, put to him by the members of the circle. I was later informed that I was 'too advanced' for that particular circle and, somewhat deflated, decided to join the second circle in which another person 'channeled' an indian guide named White Feather.

So the voice, character and presence of At-Hlan, who stands about nine feet tall, developed, and has been seen and sensed by many people. He has helped and assisted individuals with their private problems, including the use of 'far memory' to study past incarnations (in Past Life readings) and, when the circle sits, to comment upon and answer questions concerning time, space and cosmic reality. It is always right to test the truth about messages and messengers, be they from the spiritual or cosmic plane of existence, and so it is interesting to note here three things about At-Hlan.

Firstly, about a year after I started to link with him I was at a friend's home and noticed she had a book about the 'life readings' of Edgar Cayce, that great American healer, on the theme of reincarnation. Upon borrowing the book I was pleasantly shocked to discover that, about three fifths through the book, "Atlan" was described as the brother of an Atlantean prince and, near the end of the book, "the house of Atlan" was one of the families that colonised Egypt towards the end of the Atlantean dynasty.

Secondly, At-Hlan has been seen, clairvoyantly, by myself and others, in a circle, to have been initiated into the White Brotherhood. The White Brotherhood are, if you like, extra-terrestrial beings from another civilisation who are a powerful influence upon the evolutionary cycle of the earth, and therefore the spiritual progress of mankind, who were in existence before the earth was formed and indeed, were an influence in its formation. They may arrive at a circle meeting in numbers, to simply stand and observe and, although they may bring protective power against negative influences, they are basically neutral. However, information they receive may be passed to other cosmic influences and so a network may be established.

At-Hlan is a spiritual entity who has been 'promoted' (through initiation) to be able to receive and direct cosmic influences, therefore he stands as it were at the super-astral level, able to communicate with the spiritual and cosmic planes of influence and has brought other extra-terrestrial influences from the Siriun and

Polarian systems and from further afield.

Thirdly, we are fortunate enough to have psychic artist (Patsy Sellers) present in our circle who has drawn my guides and those of many other people, without any difficulty, by sensing them (clairsentience) rather than by seeing them objectively and clairvoyantly. I have been delighted by the skills and accuracy of this artistic medium. At one time I sat quietly to focus on one of my guides - an African masai warrior - without giving the psychic artist any information concerning this particular entity. She drew him in detail that was evidential and absolutely convincing and she has drawn At-Hlan on two separate occasions with only minor differences in the finished picture.

I believe At-Hlan uses me to help those who wish to know about and understand Truth, and that he is capable of communicating what might be termed Cosmic, or Universal, Consciousness. I have no doubt that he exists and can explain how the past, present and future exist simultaneously as well as what part the immortality of the human soul has to bear upon the evolution of the universe.

When reviewing the transcriptions it is fascinating to discover that there is a great cosmic influence upon the earth at present that seems to be building at an increasing rate, so that more people are beginning to experience channeling - both from spiritual and cosmic sources - and many are drawn into a network of communication that begins to answer the basic questions such as "Who is God?" and "What are we doing here?"

It is apparent from the readings that the present cosmic influences or vibrations are similar to those which existed during the high cultures of Atlantis and Egypt and that, if we so choose, we may 'tune in' to this spiritual or cosmic network at this moment in our evolutionary cycle, to discover, to a fuller degree, how the universe works and the part we may play in it. It would appear that we have a plethora of emotions - aspects of love, that are not available in such vast quantities to other planetary beings because, by and large, however advanced they may be they are products of an environment with a specific pathway to follow.

We misuse and misinterpret the power and energy that thoughts of love, support and sharing can have in the progression of our lives and so turn them around to become hate, envy and jealousy. It is important for the individual to walk along the pathway of light, for this gives us the opportunity to empower others to take charge of their lives and to become positive and secure in the knowledge that we are all playing a supportive role in assisting with the evolution of the human soul.

It seems a strong possibility that we do not necessarily expand knowledge and understanding, and hence soul growth, by only reincarnating upon the earth plane, but that we have cosmic or universal knowledge through having experienced lives upon such star systems as Sirius, Vega, Arcturus and Polaris. In fact At-Hlan states that we have twelve star influences upon this plane that form our network of direct communication, and that the spiritual and cosmic influences of the sun, together with Alpha Centuri, makes thirteen - the latter being a lucky number!

Reincarnation is a 'fact of lives' (having worked with many past life readings) so that we return time and time again to experience different cultures and differing circumstances, from humble beggar to powerful lord, and so increase our understanding of what makes mankind 'tick' and learn the niceties concerning right and wrong. This school of learning here on earth should prepare us for more responsibility at a planetary or cosmic level as we aspire to move up the spiritual ladder.

But the plan seems to have gone wrong, on the face of it, for instead of peoples of different races (therefore different cosmic influences), cultures and backgrounds learning from each other and participating together as the family of man, all from the same spiritual source, there have come about great divisions influenced by religious, political and socio-economic circumstances. We are supposed to see all people - black, brown, red, white, yellow - as our brothers and to understand, as we live on this small speck of dust way out in the galaxy, that we must unite and play our part in the development of the universe.

We have freedom of choice under universal law (God's plan) either to assist in the harmony, balance and growth of the cosmos or, once again, to reject the importance of our place in the overall scheme of things and to descend into internicene warfare and acts of degradation. Of course, mankind will evolve eventually, but at what price and at what speed and how many souls will be left behind because they have had so many chances and refused to learn the lessons of so many lives? That seems to be the point; do a certain number of souls evolve because they 'shine the light' by opening the mind to possibilities (as has been done by individuals and groups since time immemorial) or do as many people as possible use this cosmic energy at this time to help as many souls as possible to evolve and find their pathway of progression? In some ways the process by which we 'find ourselves' and help others to acknowledge the network of universal truth is the simple affirmation of allowing the spark of God within each individual to link with the great Creative Mind that is without. By unstintingly tuning in to universal love we communicate with universal knowledge and, therefore, when we ask a question we will find the answer.

At-Hlan has answered all the questions put to him in our circle, sometimes with pauses as he listens to others' advice, and he has gone to much trouble in bringing evidence of the past and of the future (hundreds of light years away) to focus our minds on the present circumstances in our evolutionary cycle or spiral. He has been the facilitator or catalyst in bringing many beings from far distant planetary systems to speak to us and has made sense of even the recent mountainous material that was hurled at Jupiter. (This was part of the influence in the evolution of that planet that has influenced us on the earth by affecting its electro-magnetic field and allowing more minds to open to the part that we are to play in universal understanding).

I am sure that At-Hlan has worked (and continues so to do) to make sense of our being, to understand the "I am that I am", but will never take away freedom of choice, as we must make our own decisions. He has only one great prophesy, which is that the year 2,000 AD will pass quietly but the years from 2,012 AD to 2,016 AD will bring about great changes upon the earth and then many more will be given the opportunity to dispense with the idea that gross materialism brings happiness and start to share in the wealth of opportunities the universe has to offer to us and we to it.

We are not pawns in some cosmic conspiracy but, given that we aspire to have dominion over ourselves, to be able to take charge of our lives, to link into universal love and to feel the mind of God working at the very centre of all things, then we have the ability to play our part fully in the universal plan; we may aspire to become Cosmic Masters through selfless acts and sacrifice, and be a step nearer to the giver of all life and all love.

10

NOTES

There are various references in the book which will need explanation here.

At-Hlan frequently refers to me as Rohann, which name seems to link with both the Atlantean era and again in a Celtic (Irish) incarnation around 800 AD; no doubt further explanation will follow as we extend the network of communication.

Some information gathered for the content of this book was collected first from the White Feather Circle and then from my own home circle and from three more public meetings as a result of meditation and channeling work done with those groups. The core of information was accumulated from a small group set up specifically to question At-Hlan over a period of two years and which gave focus, direction and a more logical sequence to the unfolding story of our existence. Although the names of several different questioners tend to be scattered throughout the book, rather than a cohesive few, we think that it gives the reading a more personal flavour instead of using 'Q' to replace the names.

In this earlier circle Azgar, a Siriun, also started to communicate through channeling and always brought almost tangible, loving energies with him. He invoked humour and laughter whilst at the same time having a serious part to play in the transfer of cosmic knowledge. The short extract appended details his first visit to the circle in which he attempts to describe himself as seen through human eyes. We have also experienced the presence of Zargon from the Polarian system, Larial of the Vegan system and Taupu from the Capellan planetary system. We have begun to channel information from these extra-terrestrial people and, as a group, have made telepathic links with their home planets through a form of astral travel. Further details of these and other informers across the galaxy will follow in a subsequent publication - "The Friends of At-Hlan".

Finally we have appended the most exhaustive Past Life Reading, channeled for Patsy Sellers, psychic artist, for whom At-Hlan took much time and trouble due to her commitment to the home circle and for the sacrifices she has made in transcribing recorded material for "The Voice of At-Hlan".

Chapter 1

The Teachings of At-Hlan

Contents

In 1992 At-Hlan Discusses The Book to be Published, and again in 1994

Different Levels of Existence

Prophecy of Changes - 2012AD - 2016AD

Our Relationship with the Universe

Extra-Terrestrial Influences

About At-Hlan

In 1992 At-Hlan Discusses The Book to be Published, and again in 1994

AT-HLAN

We give you our thanks. I bring you greetings from the world of spirit. My name is Atlan, it is important that I spell it for you - it is At-Hlan, the name is not derivitive from the place, but I come from Atlantis and I come to speak to you about Universal Truths.

You see that when we bring you greetings from the Spirit World, it is not as such as you would have on the Earth Plane. Within it is contained Truth ,within it is contained dynamic spiritual energy and power which is given to all who would sit in these circles, and this means to say that this energy is valuable to you and all on the Earth Plane - to mankind if you like. This is when White Feather says that you will spread to other places even if some of you, and this will happen, move away to other parts of your world. Therefore, it is important that you prepare your questions even though some questions may well follow on from the rest. Do you understand?

It is to give importance to these meetings because you will have, as White Feather has already suggested, to go very, very far to reach the levels that are being channeled in this area, and this is because the time and the place is correct.

It is a very serious undertaking, although of course, should be approached with humour and lightheartedness, with song, because this is what the Spirit World is - what we home in on if you like. Does this make sense to you? So when you come prepared with your questions, we will be able to answer them, have no fear about the depth of your questions, they will always be answered but we wish to make it meaningful so that you have recordings. Remember that Spirit know of your writings and recordings, and you have been told that they will be in book form to be published. There will be part of those words which will be for ordinary people, but also those words for people of this moment who wish to know of these Spiritual Truths, more depths. The last visit I made to you was rather beyond the control of my Medium, and he said that it nearly blew his psychic centres! This week we are under more control and to introduce myself there would be a space here to ask questions about Atlantis, and the world that existed before your world.

At-hlan makes reference to the previous week when he channeled through me, quite unexpectedly, and I tried to stop his energies thinking it would be embarrassing in front of strangers. In the event he refused to be forestalled and channeled with so much uncontrolled energy that his voice caused the walls to vibrate and left me quite exhausted. In the intervening week we worked together and 'matched' much more precisely. As I became more attuned to his energy and vibration then, not only teachings became evident but humour, sensitivity and thoughtfulness - all the ingredients of a well-rounded, confident and evolved 'human' being.

AT- HLAN

It is very pleasant to meet with you again. It is very important for us to meet like this, for I have been told by others upon the Spiritual and Cosmic planes of existence at this time it is important to bring knowledge to others. As well you know a pathway, a network has been set up so 'The Voice of At- Hlan' may be published. This will bring Truth to many people especially those who do not see the links between the different levels of existence. There has been little reported in terms of writing about the relationship of this planet with both the spiritual and the cosmic levels of being. I mentioned briefly in your circle meeting last, that had you passed from your Earthly bodies at that particular moment in time then you would have been linked into the Cosmic level of existence. Not only because you would have had Cosmic experience before, which is necessary, but because you have imprinted upon your super-conscious mind knowledge and information that would be valuable to the rest of the Universe. You would have for a time existed on the spiritual plane, to calm down, settle and adjust to that new, or old, way of existence. Your skills and talents would have taken you after that time, to re-immerse yourself in contacting and being a channel, part of the network with other beings from other planets.

This passage was written approximately two years after the first passage and by this time we had arrived at the fact of the inter-connectedness of all planes of existence, given the circumstances, and here At-Hlan relates that had one of us (or all) 'died' whilst meditating and channelling at a deep level then the released spirit would have been linked to a cosmic rather than spiritual or astral plane of existence.

Different Levels of Existence

AT-HLAN

I bring you greetings from the world of Spirit, it is pleasant to be with you again. I would ask you to consider yourselves, who you are, what brings you together and what you wish to bring to this circle and to the planetary plane and to the cosmic plane. For do you not know and have you not been told that the Universe, the galaxies run on the vibration of Love, from the very maker himself of itself, from that force which is around you and within you. You are many beings, you are beings from the past, you are making your being in the present, you will project this being into the future. All life is continuous, there is no cessation, it goes on infinitely, Spirit is infinite and if you bring in your present dogma then you will cease your progression, you will be involved in those things which are of the Earth. So I will quote you from one of your texts, 'Judge not lest you yourself be judged', I say this not so that you feel that you have been making the wrong decisions but that you are here to put Love into your world and therefore do not bring down your own vibration by trying to work out who should be punished and why they should be punished. For as has been said, those who commit evil against others and against themselves will have their own divine retribution, their own progress will be slow. They will be faced with the results of their own ill judged attempts to be on this Earth plane and not with all that which is good in this planetary sphere. This has been said in many different ways, but it is good to re-emphasise this, for you will find this in the teachings of At-Hlan and others who have been brought to this circle and who indeed stand within and without this Circle of Light.

Let me emphasise the Circle of Light, if you come to this circle in judgement of others then there will be very little you can do in your own progression and that of others in your planetary plane. The era of turbulence which we have spoken about, which is of this particular time, certainly of this particular year (1993) and several years to follow, really is about Love and the lack of Love. It is about people who have lost their way, it is about a lack of guidance, it is about a lack of moral stamina, it is about ways of tuning in. For your society, in this recent history, have found ways of punishing people and are beginning to find out that it is not the punishment that puts people back on the pathway of peace and harmony but of trying other ways that have been started in your own country and other countries at the moment. It is about integrating people, of showing them the error of their ways by employing them, advising them and counselling them. This indeed will be the way of the future in the next millenium, for it is not just the imprint of the past of these people that have been triggered, the adverse paths which we all have had but also the influence of those around them and the environment in which they live. So it is not just the evil deed of the one person that you have before you, but, a community of adverse effects. So, it is a learning time, not all of this is evil, although this may be apparent only at the time for this is what the media report.

You must remember that there are many learning situations upon the earth plane, there are many Temples of Light cast across the world who are working on these problems. This is one of the reasons why you join together in love with spiritual and cosmic friends to increase that spiritual and cosmic input. This is why those people gather here when they see this light being extended upward and outward. I would like to say one more word about who you bring to these meetings, for you are multi-faceted beings. There is good and bad in every single being on the earth plane and of course, if you strive to improve that which is good in you, if you strive for the path of love, forgiveness and charity, then this will overwhelm those adverse influences that you have in your past and your present and this will shape your future incarnation and the work that you do in the spiritual and cosmic plane, whichever plane you will be working on, whether it is the Astral or the Etheric or the Super-Astral, whichever plane you have aspired to, all that you have soared up to, as it were, in yourself and used with others will be taken into account.

Although we would say, do not look back over your shoulder to see what bad things or evil things you have done, the important learning factor is that you recognise that you can do far more good, if you so strive, than evil and so help this planetary system. It is not to pick out situations as you have done, in their minutiae, whether it is the death of one person or the war in Bosnia, or the starving in Somaliland, but that you send out your thoughts at this level that all people will seek towards what is the best within them, wherever they are, whatever colour or creed or background. So that, in a sense, the vibration gets raised and the awareness of all is increased and so you increase that positive karma within them , so that in the next incarnation they will stand in good stead having increased those positive aspects.

So life continues on the upward spiral and does not stultify or degenerate into the speculation of evil matters, which of course, will halt or slow the progress of the spirituality of the earthand the beings on this living planet. This creative force here which you begin to realise is as such and that there is a symbiotic relationship between the spirit earth, your spirit, the spiritual dimension and the cosmic dimension, nothing stops, all is one continuity. These teachings are very important because they strike at the very reason you are here, the reason why you are brought together, for within each of you is that spark which is wishing to be set alight and to reach out to the Solar Logos which is in control of this area of your planetary system. Of course, that person you call your God is also in a sense a minutiae of larger beings who control and organise larger areas of the cosmos, of the galaxies, and so on and so forth, that reaches out and out. So even though you may be less than a grain of sand or speck of dust within this system, you are an important part nevertheless, for all things inter-relate and perhaps your past, in the relationship between things, is more important than you would give it thought to.

This advice, given early in the sittings, is a warning against the misuse of power to promote trivial personal ambition and negativity while at the same time guiding numbers of the circle towards posotove commitment to the highest ideals. At-hlan also goes some way in explaining that when we work towards our own development we begin to experience many levels of being and begin to make sense of and integrate with Universal forces and communication networks of which we may be a part if we so choose.

Prophecy of Changes - 2012AD - 2016AD

AT-HLAN

There are things of great importance to tell you, but first do you bring your psychic powers for the development of the Circle and therefore the development of all, or are you tempted to use your power as individuals for your own use? That is the question for you to ask yourselves.

There is such a thing called prophecy, all the religious works from different time in creation have been built on the seers and the works of prophets. I come to tell you at your meeting this evening that you will see great changes in what you term the western world. There will be a temporary breakdown in liason between the countries, that you have started already to see and it will not be until mankind shares its beneficience of the world that there will be true peace in what you term the western culture. In other words it is only when those starving people are fed that the handicapped people are given their place in the world, that there will be true peace and equality. You will experience some form of chaos during the next 10 years but do not let this dissuade you from the work you are doing. This is brought about by the making of mankind.

We are telling you not to be dissuaded, not to have fear in your hearts because you are protected in more ways than you deem possible. It has been said that the year 2000 will be of great importance and this if not so. The year 2000 will pass with nothing unusual or strange happening. But if we take you forward to the year 2012 and 2016 then the world will shake her shoulders, then will you see the drift of the plates upon the planets surface. Then you will see the explosions and volcanoes and eruptions and storms and subsidence of certain parts of the world. This is spoken for you from the Super Astral who know that this is inevitable. But again we ask you to be secure and harmonious and happy, this is given to you as a prophesy from the highest plane but is is not meant to be frightening. It is for you to come to terms with your environment and your world. Indeed because you have this knowledge you will at such time be finding a increase in your powers and many other people will come to listen to your words and read your books. At this time people will lose their religious faith and religious fanaticism. So that there will be times of great upheavals both to do with the great manna that people pray to, by the money system, which they store up, and they will come to realise the uselessness of this which does not cause happiness. They will come to ask for guidance and you will find many people sobbing and weeping and praying and it will have no answer to their prayers because they have no spiritual knowledge. This is given to you to use in the future to be written down. Before this time you will have great knowledge of what goes on in the planetary systems beyond your own. Many of you by this time will have been astral travelling to other planets in your system and will find out what work goes on there and what is undertaken. This will in fact be important for what you call freedom of choice because it is your choice to become involved with this great responsibility.

You are not alone of course there are many groups who work along the same lines and with whom we have links. Indeed you will find you will have links with these groups on the astral and mental planes. This will be of great excitement to you and upliftment as well. This is all we have to say for the moment. Be of good cheer. We are not bringing you doom and gloom, but information, that you may use in the future. This underlines the importance of the work in which you are involved. Does this make sense to you? This is why also it is written that the past is the past and it is the future in which you should become involved. Do you understand?

Death and destruction is not being preached here (anyway, could it be worse than at present when two thirds of the world population is starving and there are so many wars, terrors and destruction?) but rather geophysical changes that will underline changes in social, economic and political structures. The only specific dates that are repeated several times by At-Hlan are the years 2012 - 2016. At the moment, he makes no further prophecies except, later, to detail some of the changes that many of mankind will undergo such as telepathic communication with beings from other star systems, which has been accomplished many times by all members of the circle and with members of other circles.

Our Relationship with the Universe

We wish to speak of communication. It is a more complex subject and a problem at the moment at this time on the earth plane. It is to do with your thoughts because your thoughts have energy and energy has direction and carries, like your computer, minute pieces of information with it. There is a sphere, if you can imagine it, which envelopes the planet earth beyond the pull of gravity. This sphere has intelligence, this sphere is one which can help raise the spiritual vibration, although it cannot make things happen of it's own accord. The thoughts that you have as mankind affect this psychosphere, as it has been named, and this can have a negative effect. You may have heard of the harmony of the planets, the music of the spheres. The planet sounds a note, a harmony, if this is disrupted it will effect the vibration and the note and the harmony of the other planets. Your planet is effected by signals from millions of light years away. Indeed, there are beings who are in control of this process. I have said before, your planet and it's people are perhaps the most important of God's creation, even though there are beings of more superior evolution and knowledge, they do not have the freedom of choice, the potential to reorganise the Universe for better or worse. This is why your circle is so important. This I know is difficult information to absorb but I hope that your questions will help to clarify the points I have made. There is also the effect upon the Aura and the spiritual energy that is fed from the solar energy into your solar body which effects your physical body and it's aura. I told you, it is quite complicated!

We are, each of us, guarding lives effecting the harmony of the world, there are many negative vibrations at the moment on the Earth plane, but this is being dealt with because the majority of people live their lives in peace and contentment and in Love. It is love that is the strength of a vibration, it is love that links you together telepathically and all have the potential ability for this gift, even though it may not be developed fully it is what you would call the 6th sense. Highly developed it can feed information from one incarnate spirit, that is yourselves, across the world to be received by another. The instant it is sent so your mass thoughts, including peace and harmony, do indeed effect the vibration of the earth and the note and harmony that it sends out across the cosmos.

KERRY

Are the astral and the super-astral able to work in harmony?

AT-HLAN

There are a multitude of aspects on many different wavelengths, may I say that I have been in the honoured position of being able to link the Astral and Cosmic, so that those who have experience of earthly incarnations of a higher astral experience, who have worked through suffering and experience become more refined, shall we say, then we find naturally there are links with cosmic entities. Not all these entities are good influences, some are not good, so even at that level there are choices to be made. When the initiation happens then we are able, as you suggest, to link both cosmic, super astral, astral and even as you have found out through my Brother Rohann, to look at past lives, for there is a great coming together for this is necessary to further evolution of the soul awareness of mankind.

CAROL

What is the difference between Cosmic Force and Spiritual Force?

AT-HLAN

The spiritual force has been written for you, but we would underline that we are working here on two different planes if you like in two different types of dimension. The spiritual plane comprises of those who have been incarnated on the earth, have grown again in power and are guardians of your planet and its harmony. Also at a certain level, at a higher height if you like, they link with those people from Sirius and Ursa Minor and other planetary systems, which are what you would term extra terrestrials who were here at the beginning to start the evolution of mankind. So in a sense we are all related, you are all related and we, of the extra terrestrial dimension, are related to the spiritual dimension. There will be different information, not information that argues one against the other, but information, positive information, from both the spriritual plane and what has been learned there, and from the cosmic plane and what information awaits for you to be received from that dimension.

CAROL

Are you saying that the cosmic plane is higher than the spiritual plane?

AT-HLAN

No, I would not state any sort of hierarchy at all because at this level all entities work together towards the harmony and evolution of mankind. They work in different ways and they have different kinds of knowledge to bring to bear upon the situation. Does that make sense to you? If it does not please ask me because it is very important at this stage that you understand. Please do not be embarrassed by your questions.

It becomes clear that the spiritual realms or Spirit World is a dimension closely associated with the evolution of the 'human' soul and therefore with reincarnation and living our many lives upon this planet earth. It is not a universal phenomenon. Extra-terrestrials may live, by our time, millions of years and undergo certain changes depending upon their initial environment, their own progress and therefore their actual and potential responsibilities.

Extra-Terrestrial Influences

DAVID

Do all the Extra Terrestials have more understanding of their spiritual selves or are they like earth people - only a few have understanding at this time?

AT-HLAN

Certain Extra Terrestrials have an understanding of how the whole of the cosmos works to a large degree or at least that part of the Cosmos which is pertinent to the development of life on the Earth plane and how the Earth and it's development fits into the pattern that was created for it. You can change that pathway by making the wrong choice, so these influences go back in time for millions of years, they are the White Brotherhood, for want of a better name. They are here now and will keep their eye on those beacons of light that can be shared by both the spiritual and the cosmic beings to bring about an acceleration in learning. You see, in your brain there are parts that can be attuned to this, parts that for thousands of years have not been used, or have been misused and we wish to spark this part of the brain into life, it is part of the creative flow, it is God given, it comes from your Spiritual Creator.

DAVID

Are everyday extra-terrestrials more aware of their spiritual selves than earth people over there or are only a select few more aware?

AT-HLAN

There are spiritual beings of a very high state and purity. They have such a wide experience and depth of knowledge that they have chosen to remain in and around the earth plane to help with the further evolution of mankind, so that those of you who wish to use that spiritual power through your psycic senses may use it for the betterment of mankind. If it were to be used in any other way, you as a channel would be closed down immediately and you would never find the link again, at least not in your present life, although there may possibly be opportunities sometime in the future in thousands of years, so your personal evolution is important to us. The extra-terrestrials have acknowledged that it is difficult to express that how the earth, why the earth, was formed, why the planetary systems were formed. They were part of the formation of that whole system, there are others of the same origin that have other work to do in the cosmos which is nothing to do with Earth directly, although everything in the cosmos has it's links and they have a very high field of cosmic energy that may be usedtogether with spiritual energy to help the future development of mankind.

DAVID
If extra-terrestrials can reach us from the cosmic plane why do they need to reach us in spaceships, isn't it easier for them to reach us through the cosmic plane of telepathy.

AT-HLAN
Sometimes they wish to bring a form of instrumentation which will help you with the links between the very difficult vibration of the earth plane and not just with them but from their source,as you can read if you go back to ancient civilisations. There was a direct link between people on the earth plane and the source of certain extra-terrestrials which is now lost. So we bring instruments sometimes to help to attune to this level and this channel. You will find that through this you will, indeed with much devotion,do your duty, you will be able to take this channel yourselves when the time is right. There we end. I leave you with peace and harmony.

About At-Hlan

KERRY ANNE
Well, my question is actually about yourself, because we do not really know a great deal about At-Hlan, the Warrior Priest, so when you are not being entertained by us what do you do.?

AT-HLAN
First of all this is very important work, you see for me this is the first time I have found or have been at a level of development that I can channel through a receptive being, Rohann, upon the Earth Plane. And it has taken many lives both on the Earth Plane and with Cosmic, extra-terrestrial experience to come back, to bring the knowledge and the energies of these different experiences back to you. There is a great amount of joy and happiness given and spread to the many people who communicate with me through this channel here. And so the other work that is done is still on different levels you see, on the spiritual and the cosmic, as has been said, when the light is communicated to you and you receive and add to it your energy and it is sent out unconsciously for you there are beings who are 'soul saved' as you say, because as the light shines other beings I know, your guides and other guides, come in to help those people on the pathway of destiny and progression and remove them from the lower realms of the Earth Plane. Also, you see, the stars vibrate ,the beings come in here and they are uplifted for you are all inextricably mixed at different levels in your progression.

All this work has to done by beings of , you might say, of a high calibre, who are totally selfless, who are totally committed, who are able to take their responsibilities. And so indirectly they 'sing' at a higher note, they may show their evidence through bringing guides, through healing, through bringing spiritual beings here,and I do not mean those beings who come to you from the higher Earth Realms that you see in your spiritual sittings, but those at a much higher level beyond that. And so all this work is going on all the time and we have reached a stage where we need no rest, as it were, because we feed off energies, are given energies and channel energies that are given freely from the Great Creator.They come to us through time and space and through all these systems. The nearest I can explain to you is electo-magnetic energy which at the lowest level was channelled through your Earth lines and was used in the pyramids and certain places upon the earth plane they are still used for cosmic comings and goings and communications. All that is taking place simultaneously in the wink of an eye, as it were.

And so I come to you in this form and this shape, and if you look at the moment we know that you sense my presence and my being here very powerfully this afternoon. You may see my Atlantean form and shape which goes back many hundreds of thousands of years in Atlantis and because I have had many Atlantean incarnations as well as many others, we come to you because it was a time in my lives of great energies, great understanding and of great purpose. And so this is how I present myself to you. I could come in many other forms and shapes but this is one I have adopted for it has meaning in my life and also at the time it has helped my channel to progress, and to know of Atlantis and Lemuria or Mu that was before it. And so it removed a hurdle in his progression so that he may pass that information on to others like yourselves who wish to know of such things of the earths evolution and evolution upon the earth plane. But in a sense, you see, that is a beginning. Also I come in this form as you see me, about 9 feet tall as the Brother Jonathon has said, because I come on behalf of many other beings who use this energy. So I come as an energy field, and energy force to spread the light, knowledge and information to you all.

IRENE
How many previous incarnations have you had?

AT-HLAN
This is quite a complex question, in as much as I have had many incarnations in Atlantean times. also Egyptian times, times of high culture on the earth plane. I bring myself forward to present myself to you as Atlantean, for at that time there was a high culture, a similar vibration to that which now permeates the aura and influence of the earth plane. You would say also that I am Altairean, that my home planet is Altair, and in that system also comes the spirit influence of the Dolphin for example. My number of incarnations have been many, not be too precise, over 100 incarnations upon the earth plane, and incarnations upon Altair, also upon Sirius and Polaris and other Star systems. So, I have the knowledge both of the influences that effect the Earth plane and a profound knowledge of the struggles and successes of those souls upon the earth plane both in the past and in the present

The exciting information contained withion these revelations are that there seems to be no specific, succinct earthly or spiritual system of progression to which we are bound inextricably, but that, depending upon our own past choices and the experiences that follow, we may have had incarnations upon other planets, which is explained as the story unfolds. When we work to extend consciousness then we can begin to feel a release from orthodoxy and dogmatic religious beliefs and to realise that as cosmic beings we have important work to do here and now that can positively effect the progression of the 'human' soul as we make stronger links with those extra-terrestrial influences and communicators who wish to assist the evolutionary cycle of the earth at this particular time.

HANNAH

You have said you exist on a super Astral Level, do you know the Council of Nine collectively or individually. You yourself must need to go home to recharge after working with the Earth or other missions. How often do you need to do this - to relax and confer with other beings?

AT-HLAN

I am empowered with much energy. I use this particular channel (Rohann) because we are in tune and we have met before and the voice of this channel is not unlike my voice when I was on the Earth plane, although I was bigger in the build and the voice volume was three times the volume of my channel. I find it very pleasant and easy to work with through this channel. When I need to recharge energy, as it were, it is very simple, I return to my place of residence and sit quietly and meditate as you do upon the Earth plane, although sometimes when I meditate I do pick up telepathic signals from my channel and also from those associated with him in your circles. That is quite a complicated network that I will not go into detail at this time, but again I will at another time. You are asking where my residence is, for you see there are may places. It is easy for me to say I return to the Spirit World, I return to a different level, a different plane of existence, not the next dimension that you visit when you first pass over as they say. In fact that is not in itself true for those of you who die in the earthly body do not all necessarily just go to the Spiritual dimensions for some of you are Avatars, some of you have Cosmic connections.

Sometimes it is a point of frustration when you sit clairvoyantly and ask for a person to return and they cannot be called for they have gone to another dimension, another world if you like, for, as you were saying earlier Kerry-Anne, the whole thing is more complex than you would imagine. So I go, as I have said, to my Super Astral plane. Now, I could refer you to the book that my channel has been reading by the Lady Geraldine Cummings who was an Autonomist. She channeled a gentleman called F.W. Myer who had investigated the different planes of existence or progress. So, I have progressed to what we would call the 6th dimension; after saying that you may look it up; in other words, there is a more rarified atmosphere where I have my residence, it is not the 7th dimension which is the Chohan, the highest Avatar, but I have rarified existence and I am able because of this to tune into both the Cosmic and Spirit planes. In a sense I am cosmic rather than Spiritual although I have lived many times upon the earth plane in may different forms, shapes, sexes and places. I have if you like carried my burden, overcome much negativity and have been allowed to aspire, you would say, to greater things, to a greater depth and breadth of influence and therefore responsibility. I could carry on further Lady Hannah but I think I have answered your question sufficiently, is that so?

HANNAH
Yes, thank you.

A QUESTION was asked about whether At-hlan and White Feather, working at different vibrations, actually sensed and communicated with each other.

AT-HLAN
We communicate, White Feather and I, as you are aware from time to time and he lightens my vibration very, very frequently. So you see, the teachings are for a dual purpose, the writings are for a dual purpose and this is important for it is not often in the past or present that this has been done for the Astral and the Super Astral, neither has it been brought to peoples attention that there have been communications between different entities working on different wave lengths, wherever they are, and it has been a surprise to my channel and other people in the circle that this can be accomplished through your commitment and through searching for the Truth and bringing this into your lives.

PATSY
I would like to ask you At-Hlan, about the people around you, the ones you

confer with, could you tell us a little more about them please?

AT- HLAN

You will certainly find out more about them as we progress in the Circle. This is another reason why, for a time, you will find my influence there rather than here. For I am allowed to confer with many beings on a cosmic level. The White Brotherhood have allowed this communication to take place for you. We have also got communication from the spiritual realms as well, those great spirits who come to you such as White Feather and Red Cloud, but I will not say too much upon this subject because you will find others from the spiritual plane who come to meet you, to greet you and to bring their teachings. I wish not to pre-empt those meetings but of course on the Cosmic level there are the Great Beings from different Star Systems with whom I communicate when I am unsure. Infact, I had thought that I would not be allowed to give such depth and breadth of information. We are allowed to do this for it is important at this time for the progress of many on the Earth Plane, which is why we have said earlier that we wish this to be written and for the book to be published. Even though my channel does not know how or where or when it will be published.

PATSY

Like a 'test of Faith'!!

AT- HLAN

Perhaps it is not so much a test of faith but a test of the influences that we may bring to bear with those who have the Faith, the Beliefs and the Knowledge. Faith without knowledge and understanding is mindless leading to dogma and creedalism.

By committing ourselves and widening our fields of consciousness and awareness, through different pathways of progression, through meditation, then, in a way, the energies and power that we generate set up vibrations that attract guides to us. By the general use of the term 'guides' we may include those beings from the spiritual planes of existence (sometimes referred to as astral planes) and those beings who have progressed to what is often termed (by At-Hlan) as the super-astral plane, many of who have had both earthly and extra-terrestrial incarnations. The third category of 'guides' are the extra-terrestrial visitors, with whom At-Hlan often has contact, who have been seen by many in the home circle and who channel information from a source of light years distance from earth.

Chapter 2   ***Difficulties of Soul Progression***

Contents   About Pain and Suffering

Adverse Influences

The Effects of Dis-ease

Progression and the Power of Love

The Influences of Healing

About Pain and Suffering

KATHLEEN
Why do some people suffer so much pain in their life?

AT-HLAN
There are many reasons why people suffer because there are adverse forces where there should be love and light, there is darkness and anger, a perversion of love. Always there is a struggle upon the earth plane as well as on the cosmic level. Sometimes you may become a focus of attention for these adverse forces. Your life will be influenced by that and most unfortunate indeed, as it were, as this happens the angels weep. Always this is counterbalanced by further and higher experiences by that person, although I realise at the time it does not help a great deal. Sometimes the persons themselves will choose the wrong pathway. Always there are beings of light who stand ready to help but sometimes they are not seen, the presence is not called for and so some people suffer very greatly.

In that learning situation they learn at an enormous level in another life on the spiritual plane and reincarnation on the earth plane to understand humanity at a great depth. It is a great learning for them and because you have freedom of choice we cannot stop people from choosing the wrong pathway, all we may do is provide beings of light near them who will help when they are called upon. Also, some people have actually chosen in their incarnation to suffer. It is their way of atoning for they have made others suffer. Some beings will incarnate for a short period of time because that is their learning experience in that incarnation. You see, there are may different influences that flow in and around an incarnation upon the earth plane.

Adverse Influences

JILL
Could you please explain how illness, pain and suffering progresses the human soul?

AT-HLAN
This has been a much mistranslated problem with the evolution of the physical body. Originally you were not meant to suffer on the physical plane but you were meant to learn from various inputs and influences, because the whole progress has been uncorrect.... that is not the right word.... because the progress of mankind has been changed. There is a learning situation for those who have to deal with those who are mentally ill, physically retarded, those who are in pain and suffering and indeed it maybe said that this is part of the reason that those people chose to incarnate upon the earth plane and to finish their lives in such a manner, because it evokes a form of love and caring. On the other hand things have gone awry for there are also influences of karma from past lives and influences that are man-made that effect the environment, the ozone layer and pollution and so on, which also effect the cell structure.

KERRY
Greetings to you At-Hlan. It has been said that as a human progresses spiritually then the physical body suffers is this correct? If so can you explain why and advise us on how to protect our nervous systems. *(Communicated at the Summer Solstice 1993).*

AT-HLAN
You see it was all very well for the Yogi in his cave where he could progress for himself and very often for others on the Earth plane, needing no protection, but when you are in a world populated by men and women and you have your daily contacts, verbal and physical contacts, then you become more sensitive and aware in your development of positive influences and adverse influences. If you are surrounded only by those who are of higher thought, who are committed to the light then there are no problems. When we are surrounded by a mixture of energies/forces, then our beings, our different bodies, can be affected. And so in your case, Lady Kerry-Anne, on a mental level you have been affected by

negative influences. So it is good in your meditation to ask not just for protection for that time but throughout your daily life. Of course this will not always be 100% because your defences are sometimes lowered. In your case by the anger you feel, the remorse and guilt you feel concerning your children and those around you that you love and care for. But always in your meditation take the white light and wear this throughout the day and occasionally pause to reinforce it, and take that white light and put it around you very tightly from your feet right up to your crown centre. This will help but there is no absolute answer to this problem of existence because that is precisely what it is throughout our lives. We are weighed down by our thoughts, problems and responsibilities for ourselves and as we progress increasingly for others. Even the Master Jesus had moments of weakness when he found himself suppressed and depressed by the weight of his responsibilities. So if it can happen to a Cosmic Master so then it can happen to those who aspire to such heights as of course we all do, for there is no limit to our progression only that which we surround ourselves with. They are barriers which we put up against our own progression. Of course we realise that those barriers are not always self-imposed they are sometimes imposed by others and, for example, this is a good time for one member of this circle to make a strike for freedom, to use the power which is around. We all have our personal responsibilities and our trials and tribulations to overcome. In the case of my channel Rohann we know he has many strong beliefs and many gifts, but he has times when he feels that the world has deserted him although this does not last for too long a period of time. We all have moments of doubt, moments of weaknesses but let us be assured that the work that we do between us is listened to and appreciated by those at the very highest level of existence.

The network grows and those who listen, who tune in, who pick up this vibration are in some cases almost enamoured of it and in some cases it removes doubt for some who even at a high level taken their gifts, their talents elsewhere for they would have felt rejected. And so what you build up is a network that includes more and more people into this ever finer vibration which is sent out upon your behalf in this direction. It is important for you to know that none of this work is wasted even if it is not written, it is recorded. It is calculated by many at a high level and we ourselves have listened to those who would do an injustice to you and you will find for the rest of this year you are well protected and there will be no re-occurance of this illness you have felt on the mental, emotional level of your body and so all will be well with you, you may go forward as they say 'bright eyed and bushy tailed' . But still it would be a good time for your personal development, in circle and in meditation to recharge your batteries and to improve your self-image within yourself for you personally perhaps to let some time pass before your public work goes on. You will find that next year it will be easy for you and that the nervousness that you have felt will dissipate and that you will be far more confident and that there will be no interference in your work.

This is a more personal aspect of At-hlan's work which usually is done on a one-to-one basis but here he makes an exception and the advice to the medium in the circle is, simply put, "Close down your mediumship work for at least six months, recover your psychic power and just be a family person". For another member he mentions, almost in passing, that the positive energies present could help her life to become more free.

KERRY ANNE
If you were to mix with people who are very negative and who are on a low vibration could that also affect your physical well being?

AT-HLAN
When you are aware, as you all are, of those positive and negative influences that surround you, as there is always a mixture. Until we are thousands of years into the future when the negative influences have been neutralised gone as you say back to square one to relearn their lessons, until such time you will have to cope with that which surrounds you and when you overcome the negative influences then you grow yourself. And so it is not always a bad thing because in overcoming these negative influences very often you can empower other people with love and care and this is a test of your true beliefs. Also that those who would do you harm that you feel strong enough, and I emphasise when you feel strong enough, to turn the other cheek then you lift others and in lifting others you grow yourself.

But you have reached the stage all of you at this point in time when you are able to stand strong and make your decisions based upon the strength of knowing that in one direction there is hope for the person and you use your positive influences to lift them and in another direction, as you say, it is wasting your time your energies and your gifts and your skills, particularity when you have tried time and time again and all has come to nothing. For others you see have their responsibilities do they not, this is important for you to know and if you have helped to open the door, to guide their footsteps along a pathway and still they are bitter and twisted and bowed down in their own lack of wishing to know, lack of wishing to progress, to be quite happy surrounded by ignorance and futility, then what is the point. The natural laws say that you should work with those where there is a possibility for progress and that you all have your limits in this direction and so you will know in your heart of hearts where there are opportunities for the light to shine for the sun to grow and lift people. Always there will be those who will not be lifted, again I will bring you to the case of the Buddha or the man called Jesus there were limits even there to what was possible because not all peoples eyes were open, not all peoples ears listened and so if you look historically at the limitations placed upon them then you will see that you have your own limitations.

KERRY
Thank you At-Hlan but we do like to tax your brain!!!

AT-HLAN
I do not mind in the slightest it is a pleasure to be of service to you.

"Why do people suffer?" is a frequently heard cry of despair, particularly when we think of 'good' or 'innocent' individuals who have apparently done nothing wrong ot evil to bring about mental imbalance or physical pain caused by disease. Rather than avoiding the issue, summarily dismissing it or directing us to 'the will of God', At-Hlan takes the questions fully on board and answers in great detail that gives us an insight into the complexities of our existence. It becomes apparent that suffering may be self-imposed (as in making atonement for causing suffering in a previous incarnation) or other-imposed, but in the longer term we learn to progress through sacrifice and giving love, especially to those who, by orthodox thinking, do not deserve to be loved. In some ways it is far more important to send loving thoughts to those who formerly we disliked, for this assists in their more positive progress and also helps our own individual progress. Therefore we have to radically change our thinking about existence in the short and long term for, logically, it is easy to love those near to us but far more difficult to send positive thoughts about those whom we consider to be evil. However, if you think about it, if all people sent out unconditional love in all directions to all people then very soon there woulod be peace on earth.

ANNE

We hear of possession and entities attaching themselves to people. Some people can become distraught, horrible and nasty things can happen to them and ruin their lives. Why is this allowed. I do not think it should be.

AT-HLAN

Well you see, it is not always a question of what is allowed but the conditions around that particular person either in this life or a past life. You are thinking in a sense in parochial terms in the space-time continuum. That person may, I suggest have been balancing his or her future pathway by experiencing those things that they have perhaps inflicted upon other people. This is a great generalisation and I realise that it is a very sensitive area for discussion and concern. It maybe they have opened themselves purposefully in this direction, it may be it has been inflicted upon them. I would beg you to think in terms of many lives and many experiences and try to remove yourselves from thinking particularly about a person with only one life at this particular time and place. This is because the whole network is far more complicated than that.

KERRY

The souls that are actually on the Earth now, the ones that are nothing more than pure negativity, the ones that instil fear in people, the ones that thrive on fear and power. Will those kind of souls be prevented from returning?

AT- HLAN

There is as you know, guidance for trapped souls who are not necessarily negative but are lost and shocked and in a state of amazement. It is because over thousands of years you have lost the ways of teaching of the Knowledge to instil into people from a very young age. Should they pass into the world of spirit very quickly or elsewhere, they would instantly understand this and so be able to cope with this teaching, this communication, this wisdom that has been lost. This is why it is now necessary for people to be able to bring in their guides and to show them the way forward to the relevant plane of destiny and progress. There are of course some negative influences among those as well , as there are negative influences or images/thought forms that have been conjured up by those upon the Earth plane which are truly there as bad influences that can affect young people as well as older people. Where the atmosphere is negative you will find this influences younger people who , I will repeat, are very open to suggestion. So they lead a life which is destructive for a time. This is not irreversible. The work that you do, and other circles do, upon the Earth plane is very important to dissolve or destroy these negative Earth forms. These images that are created purposefully in some cases to cause chaos and mayhem, .to cease, stop or slow the progress of those that they can influence. It is necessary for such circles as yours and rescue circles, to guide not punish those negative spirit forms who need guidance. They are frightened of their future, for they have not been guided when they were in the body.

HANNAH

Is there a difference between your spirit and your soul?

AT-HLAN

In a sense you have your etheric body, your spiritual body, also a mind which registers all the experiences and the mind is a contact between your soul and your brain, a bridging link. It is not part of the physical, it is a product of the electrical system of which your etheric body is finely composed. All this registers on the soul. When you die, for example, the soul and the etheric body and that spark of light you call God, which is a combination of the trio, Father, Son and Holy Spirit, that goes over to the spirit world and when you reach higher dimensions then you lose the etheric body and acquire a finer body.

HANNAH

I was wondering about earth bound spirits - I mean will they eventually be released to go on in their progressions?

AT-HLAN

This is the ultimate goal for all souls to progress to be part of the universal plan to help with the expansion of the universe to help stabilise and add harmony. For as you know many souls have been trapped for hundreds if not thousands of years and we have sent guides to allow them to progress. For like attract like and so there are many who stay close to the density of the earth plane, for they themselves are in a world of illusion. They are not progressing and this is ,as I referred to earlier, a form of intreversion for each person. There are opportunities for them to come into the light and this happens at some stage even though sometimes they may not wish it, they are not saved - that is the only way I can think of putting that, for in their way they are clogging up the system. They sometimes arrest the progress of other souls for they keep them trapped on the earth plane if they have great influence. However, one of the reasons for this new vibration which you call a cosmic vibration, this new reality, is to allow and even insist on the progress of earth bound and trapped souls so that the system maybe cleared of blockages so that at least all that wish to follow the light may do so and those who do not will be lead towards a place where they may make some decisions as to whether they are regressing, going back, or wish to go forward. These are very important choices for them to make. Have I answered that question?

HANNAH
Yes thank you - so there is hope for every soul?

AT-HLAN
Yes there is hope for every soul, it is a point of frustration that sometimes those souls who have been given instruction, guidance, the light, have sometimes still refused and so they may go to a place and ponder and see the different pathways of possibilty much more clearly laid before them. There is no universal law to say that they must progress, they still have choice and so the progress may take thousands of years to complete and so they find themselves behind the more advanced souls like yourselves who have chosen to progress, who have allowed the light to shine.

The Effects of Dis-ease

LENETTE

Will AIDS really wipe out large portions of the population?

AT- HLAN

No, AIDS is really a reflection of stress, misunderstanding, introversion and misuse of energy and so on.It is not something that will destroy large numbers of people. With the learning that comes from such a disease we have found that it has struck a chord with other people. They learn that processes are emitted with such a disease and there has been much love and understanding and care given to many people. That tends to bring about the destruction of negative thinking about certain types of people, if you understand my meaning. These people have been said to have been not of a certain persuasion or outlook, but as human beings who have suffered. There have been lessons learned about the pointless misuse of energy and aberrations of the human character that can bring about such diseases. It has been a normal process with those people. We talk about Atlanteans; there were many, many powerful and spiritual people in Atlantis civilization. You remember it was spread over tens of thousands of years. There were Atlanteans who came back who had less influences but have come back still to learn a lesson. For many of them the lesson was not learnt in Atlantis when the downfall was brought about. They learnt as individuals here that you still cannot misuse your personal power and energies because it brings about the AIDS situation. By the same token it is not that they will suffer, it is that they will learn, so in the next incarnation they will have learnt a lesson at last in this one, to use their energies, for positive and enlightening purposes.

PATSY

At-Hlan, along the same sort of lines - Kerry and I were discussing a programme she saw on television about a young girl who had Anorexia, she was literally starving herself to death, she virtually had a death wish. It seems that some people are born with this 'death wish', why would that be?

AT-HLAN

You see the simplest questions are very difficult to answer quickly. For when you are a child, a seed, you bring with you thoughts, memories of the past lives and different conditions and so also sometimes the environment that surrounded you under those conditions. You also have the conditions of your present incarnations which may positively or adversely affect you. So, it may be a combination of the past and present. For these people that suffer from Anorexia it may be mental, emotional condition. They have chosen to be here, remember that, and sometimes their condition will bring about, in those upon whom it is the responsibility to guide them, a greater sense of responsibility, it may trigger in them something that has been missing, personal responsibility, for that younger person.

Very few of these people pass into shall we say, the Spirit world, as result of this condition, although we know of some who have died in desperation because they have not found on the earth plane the spiritual upliftment that they sought and it is this side of despair that often leads them to this condition. They are not advanced souls do you see, they cannot control their own spiritual, mental and physical environment and so they take this way out so that they can return to that that they know which is one plane upon the, or in the, spiritual universe. They have not learned their lesson, by the same token it may well be that those who influence them had not learned their own lesson. But this is only one aspect of any disease, this is one in particular. Healing is of great benefit to these people for they will all feel the love that they miss and it will help them to overcome their despair, you see these people are crying inside constantly and it's a way of escaping. I think I will finish there for now (he laughs) I laugh at myself here, I was going to say 'you could write a book' about each of these questions and one reason why you have given your time unstintingly and your commitment to this work is, in fact, to write a book, in fact you are beginning to see now why it is important.

Progression and the Power of Love

KERRY

When coming into contact either with people with extremely negative vibrations, what can we do as individuals to raise their vibration, to act more positively?

AT- HLAN

LOVE THEM!! Very difficult, yet for many people that may help their progression. You see, those of you who understand part of your past incarnations, your reasons for being here, have acquired knowledge, and hopefully have acquired wisdom from that knowledge so that you will know that you are here for a reason and part of a plan. You would also know that there are those who would be destructive and aggressive and the only way to deal with those is to send them healing thoughts, which are thoughts of love. Azgar would be able to tell you much for he has worked among people upon this planet doing this kind of work. Always there are struggles, by this manner also will be your own progression. It is not always easy, but that is where wisdom is used rather than just the knowledge. Wisdom comes in at a much deeper level of understanding and given freely as love is given freely to you and for you to work with.

MAUREEN

I would like to ask a personal question, I would like to know what my life purpose is and what more can I do to tune into that.

AT- HLAN

We are not here with due respect to answer personal questions, but I can take that personal question and answer it for you and all those assembled here.

The reason for the existence of a being is progression, is to help with the evolution of that planetary system. In general terms each person on this Planet of Choice has alternatives, has a pathway which they may accept or reject. Each person has his or her personal responsibility to help for the evolutionary process which involves what you would call the human soul. Although from our perceptions it is not merely human, it is also Cosmic, for is not God, whom you call God, a Cosmic Being. The way forward, Lady Maureen, with your life is simply to get to know and understand, learn about Unconditional Love, for all things in the Universe are based on different facets of what you term Love. On this planet you have a potential excess of love, unfortunately because you have choice it is misused, misinterpreted and so instead of having charity, support, sharing and caring which are facets of love, it is turned to anger, hate and prejudice, the other side of the coin as it were. As you link in with us we would ask you not to dictate for this would take away your choice in such matters, but to ask to use this Love to the best of your potential ability. Always you have of course, what you would call, rejections, reversals, difficulties, but if you will believe us sometimes this is part of a difficult learning process. Always when love is given, even if it is rejected or perverted or interfered with in some way, always when love is given it is returned. Not always on this level of existence but on some level of existence it is returned and you progress.

The Influences of Healing

PENNY

When healing is being given can it be beneficial to the person, the instrument, giving the healing or does it deplete their energy?

AT-HLAN

There was a time when people used what is known as Magnetic Healing where they used their own energies and transferred that energy to others. This was not a good thing in many ways, first of all it drained their own energy and if, or course, there was something wrong with them they would transfer this to the patient. Spiritual healing, as you call it, or contact healing is using that power of love that I have talked about, that is everywhere. That power may be channeled through the healer to the patient. In fact, your scientists have now found that certain defence cells, as you might call them, in the healer have been accentuated, energised for a more healthy healing of the healer as well as the patient, or client or whoever this energy is being used for. For when the energy is being used it is not just a simple energy it is an energy that has many different levels depending on what is wrong with the patient. Of course, if you are a healer it depends on your own spiritual stature as to who you bring to that healing and that you may bring spiritual energy or cosmic energy or entities who wish to help. If you are a pretence of a healer who really has no energy at all, you may draw on negative energies or shells of people, or those earth bound energies who actually have no use whatsoever, you can make conditions worse. So the power of the healing very much depends on the channel that is being used for your healers are mediums who channel this power.

PENNY

So do we ask for specific healers in spirit to be with us when we are giving healing?

AT-HLAN

Whether you ask or not, for your healing energies or entities, it is quite a difficult problem because you may have spiritual healing conveyors of that force who may be formless and shapeless, but for mankind they like to see a form or a shape. Very often when you are healing, a medium who is clairvoyant, who is healing, may see a personage in shape or form for this is more consoling for the medium and sometimes for the patient.

SYBIL
Are there any amongst us who may be able to perform psychic surgery.

AT-HLAN
This also brings the question, what is psychic surgery. For healing can be done where energy is being used very often and quite commonly, to manipulate bone structures and to disperse cancerous material to rid the body of, what can I say, simply rid the body of crystals that should not be there. At the same time there has to be the mental, there has to be the soul, the soul awareness, so sometimes when healing is being done and the soul will not be shifted the healing is not efficacious or maybe transient or temporary, the soul is not in harmony with itself and with the body. We go back to the psychosomatic, if your body is not functioning properly there is a reason, the reason is generally because the soul is not at rest. The other bodies are invisible. If you could see an aura you would see breaks in it for example, or weaknesses, for it is tied up with the endocrine system and so on. So you have your etheric body and the aura and the astral body, all have to be harmonised. If these are not consistent with each other it is difficult to do a healing in any depth that will last. Now this is not so in many cases, in many cases it is simply that energy may be used on the mental body to restore the mental network of vibration which reacts with the physical body.

At the same time there may be karmic influences there from a past life, there may be influences from other people there as well who have created a negative vibration. So it is a little more complex than we, than many healers, would like to think. I do not want to be negative about this, many healings can be simple and straight forward, some are not. When you think about these things you will find that people may have the same complaint, be ill at ease or diseased in some way, you may heal one and have 100% cure of that disease, in another one it will make no difference at all, so that it is these other influences that are brought to bear, one and not the other.

HANNAH

A question of interest I think. I have heard of someone planting a healing garden and I think they used Rose Quartz and other crystals like Amethyst and some flora or shrubs, particularly sage and fuchia. They said that they did this because in case of perhaps adverse climatic cxhanges it offered their thanks to Mother Earth and also it was cloak of protection around their homes.

ATHLAN

The prime source of adverse influences may come from many different directions, they come from adverse spirits, they may come from cosmic forms, but these gardens are really tuning in love with the right amount of crystals and then they send out a vibrancy. They have to be fed by love because you can have two crystals, they might be similar but one might vibrate as if it were dead. So there has to be an inter-relationship between the person and the stones and the stones will help the growth of the plants, and the plants will rejoice for the love that has been brought into that place. So, I suppose that in a wider sense there will be an area of protection, but an area of protection that will be brought to bear because of the love brought to that place. Yes, this will be picked up by other beings at different wavelengths who will be pleased, but the main thing is not to put your crystals and your plants in and leave them, but put them in a place where you can sit and tune in when you can. Bring love from different places, from different planes of existence and the plants and the stones feel this vibrancy and this joy and so you have linked different planes of existence from the humble stone to the plants, to the animals, to the human beings, to the spirit world and so on.

This is important, particularly with a person who has esoteric knowledge and who can maximise the benefits of that healing place. It is going back to Druidic times, as it is said that stones and plants were used to cultivate earth magic and so really you are talking about earth magic, but this has far wider implications when it is done for the right reasons and by the right people who understand what they are doing, for much of this was done, as you would know, in places like Avebury and Stonehenge and so on, where a lot of Earth magic was used and animal life, but it turned around the wrong way when they had to slaughter animals and in some cases, human beings, for they were not linked with their God and being part of the love network, but thought that to appease their Gods they had to bring about pointless and needless slaughter. That is why these places were destroyed in the same way the Atlantis was destroyed before, because they perverted the use of the powers that they had.

So, your healing garden has much wider implications than you think. They say that there is nothing new upon the planet earth, well, there are some things that are new but that system goes back hundreds of thousands perhaps millions of years. So, at its best it can fill those who visit us with a very vibrant and positive outlook on life and can help to balance the energy centres in the person and can help to bring the spirit world present. The Indians of north america knew of this, the Anasazis knew of this and used these stones in special places, not complex places but special places, when they cultivated the links between different levels of being upon the Earth and the spiritual and the cosmic...such a simple question!

Chapter 3　　　*Working with the Light*

Contents　　The Work of Home Circles

　　　　　　Different Levels of Communication

　　　　　　Energy Centres or Chakras

　　　　　　Meditation and Channeling

　　　　　　I AM THAT I AM

The Work of Home Circles

IRENE
What is the best way to develop a Home Circle?

AT-HLAN
There are many ways in which you can form your home circle, which will bring people into the light and you will find that people will automatically come to join these circles, there are ways of linking into the light at an earthly level, a spiritual level and a cosmic level. When you are open to such influences they will come to you, you will be given your evidence also, maybe from a television programme, or reading a book, or talking to a person quietly, or being in a particular place at a particular time. Truths are always given to those who are open who wish to follow the pathway. So, you will build your terms of references, you will follow the path of the initiate, of the wise ones, you will find your links, you do not have to rush here, there or thus to find them when it is known the plane of Universal Consciousness, to which you are in tune, to which you are in tune at the moment, when it is know that such a person, such a circle, such a group exists for the highest reasons in particular, you will find that High Guides come to assist you with this pathway.

Unfortunately, it does not mean to say that you do not have to undergo the experiences at an earthly level, so still you will have your struggles and your battles, and your hurdles to overcome, but you will know at a heart mind and soul level that always you will have support, strength and courage when you tune into these beings at this level.

TIM
Could you tell us a little about the work that circles do and enlighten me as to what we take away when the circle is disbanded?

AT-HLAN
It depends very much at which level that circle is working. Of course there are negative circles which follow the left hand path, of course, all they take with them from that is their own lack of progression and their own darkness. Looking at it from the positive side there are circles who sit for their own soul awareness

and development and the development and soul awareness of the circle, may send their light out to others who need it on the earth plane, particularly the innocent. So they will take away with them to an extent, the knowledge and understanding of the work that they have done on a soul level. There are other people who sit in a circle for rescue work, who rescue earthbound and trapped souls that have endured shock or much negative karma, who have stayed upon the earth plane for they have not seen the light. So they sit to bring souls to them with their guides of light, through their own pathway of destiny and progression, even though some of those souls may not wish this at the present time and so progress despite their opposition.

There are other circles who will sit to increase their awareness at an earth level of the devas and the devic kingdom, of the earth sprites as they are called, of the earth spirits. The North American Indians were excellent channels at this level. So they will take away with them more understanding and knowledge at an earthly level. There are those who sit at a spiritual level, so that they can communicate with the realms of the spirit world which is just the twinkling of an eye away and so when they pass over they will not go in fear but in joy and understanding into such a plane of light that exists for them. There are those who sit at all of those levels and at the cosmic level also, in which you have been involved yourselves, and so at that level of understanding they may well incarnate, if they are sufficiently well developed, and become a higher being of light, one who works at a different planetary system in a different part of the universe. We could discuss a rather large book upon why circles sit and what the individuals take away with them in terms of knowledge and understanding, but I think this is sufficient for you to accept at the present.

Different Levels of Communication

AT-HLAN

When you sit in the circle of light a beam is sent out and many souls are attracted to this beam. It stands before them as a saving light as a place that they can focus into that will guide them to their spiritual destiny. So as you sit here there are lost and trapped souls who are finding their own pathway merely because you sit for the truth and unselfishly for others. That note and that vibration indeed cut through space further in fact than you can possible imagine that space exists. When you ask why you sit, how can you imagine the Berlin wall, which was a symbol of division between peoples, fell so quickly, or that the yoke of oppression was relieved in the Russian domain, or that apartheid begins to disappear, or more recently that the Jew and the Arab take the first step along the pathway of peace which is so important for the progression of the whole world. It is circles like yours, it is the prayers sent out, that cause these things to happen. It is not political parties, not by joining groups, who with the best intentions in the world still create waves that send out forms of dispute and dissemble the truth. So be with us overjoyed that such groups exist and do this work, not just for the harmony of this planet but for its relationships with other planetary systems in the universe.

This is why these communications are so important in such star systems as is found in Sirius and Polaris and further afield. Your mental aptitude and your soul are linked together both to receive information and to send information from all the different planes, from the material to the astral to the cosmic and you have the potential to be involved with this at a very high level. So that is why such people as Asgar are overjoyed to meet you and to bring love from that planet, others also besides your guides, those of you who have the eyes to see and the ears to hear, will see around this room if you look carefully, then you will sense, feel or see so many beings that you would not imagine they could all fit into this room. But of course for us time and space do not exist so all things are possible.

AT-HLAN

I will finish with a general teaching, a general philosophy to those who come to such circles of light, to say that, for many of you in your past lives you have linked with Atlantean or Lemurian times, you have linked with Egyptian times, often with Jewish people, at the time of Jesus, at the time of Buddha, at the time of high culture in Greece and so on, not always, but whenever soul is progressing how else does the soul progress, but at some stage in it's progression it is linked to higher cultures to assist and help that culture to grow, even in the knowledge that when that cycle is over then they will have to inhabit the body of a pauper or someone who has undergone great sacrifice. Always there is an upward spiral, always there is growth, always there is an upward evolutionary cycle so that no human being can stop that cycle, certainly it may be slowed in some areas and at other times it will be accelerated as is undergoing the earths cycle at this present time. And so, I have great joy and great humility in communicating with you and with other beings, who at the moment you cannot see, but from whom I receive my information for I am also a channel as well as a being. A being that is empowered to link both the spiritual and the cosmic planes of being.

It is certainly a new era. Whereas formerly home circle sat generally for clairvoyance, soul saving (rescue work) and physical phenomena we now have links with what might be called the 4th/5th dimensional or cosmic level of communication. And it is not 'all out there' but within us for we are part of 'all that is' as we appreciate that we have not only had many past lives here upon the earth plane but also have incarnated upon other planets, certainly within our own galaxy and perhaps further afield. If it were not so then we would be devoid of the facility of extra-sensory or telepathic perception to see, hear, sense and then to channel the information given by our extra-terrestrial friends. As a channel myself I find it quite amusing that At-Hlan refers to himself as a channel, but this must be so, as he gives much information that he has acquired but also, as a link, he passes on information from other sources in the cosmos and also helps to guide them to our circle using his energies; Channeling is, literally, universal!

AT-HLAN

I wish to talk this evening about what you call the Super-Astral, or in some cases, the Cosmic, to clear up a point of the Teaching that came through some weeks ago. It is a question in some of your minds, 'Why do extra-terrestrial entities from Sirius or Polaris, or from other Galaxies wish to channel in your circle? why do they wish to tune into this light that gets sent out on such a fine wave length through such a distance?' And the answer to that is that we all have to progress, as you progress on your level so others progress on their level under different circumstances, under different environments. Some are very advanced to such an extent that they are invisible, for they work on a higher vibration, but they are just as real in their world as you are in yours. But you do have an amount of very primitive emotional energy and I do not wish you to feel insulted by this, but in their progression some of this emotional energy has become so formalised as to lose its power of ascendancy and progression and evolution. You have such an excess of emotion, much of it used for the wrong purpose, as you find in your world at the moment, so the love that you channel into this circle and the note that is channelled with it, the harmony that it can bring may be used by those from a completely different environment.

Energy Centres or Chakras

SUSAN

I have a question about the Chakras. In the books I have read they say there are seven, but I have heard there are more, is this correct?

AT-HLAN

Well you see it depends who you are and what you are working with, towards or from. For example if you are a healer or a medium or channeling or going into trance and so on. But there are indeed the basic seven energy centres which my channel opened and you focused in upon at the beginning of this session. They are generally speaking, the most important energy centres for they are the centres which link with your etheric body. So you see if you are doing healing on the etheric body then that vibrancy of loving energy gets transferred from the etheric to the physical body. As far as my channel is concerned he recognises two of the energy centres, one above the crown which is pink/deep red magenta, for someone else there would be one at the knee, which would be brown, a very strong link with the earth; there is another one at the ankles - so you see much has been written and it is very easy to get confused. The one at the ankles, for your own terms of reference, is a very deep green colour, it is difficult to describe but my channel may be able to describe it to you as he can see it. It is rarely described by anyone who has written any books you have read. There are also energy centres in the palms of the hands and in the feet, not strong energy centres as you would call them, but sub-energy centres also, there is one at the temple. So there is a complex pattern of main centres, smaller centres and so on which when you think about it it makes sense does it not? I think I had better stop now Lady Susan.

Although this is correct it must be said that directly above the crown energy centre we have found Pluto (green/blue) which has a relationship with the extent of our conscious thought for it is furthest of the planets in our system; above Pluto is the Solar Logos, the highest centre as described above.

You may be interested in how we open our energy centres; their location and influences are listed below. We open from the base Chakra up and close from the crown centre down.

> *Red, ruled by Mars - base of the spine*
> *Orange, ruled by Jupiter - spleen centre*
> *Yellow, ruled by Saturn - solar plexus*
> *Green, ruled by Venus - heart centre*
> *Blue, ruled by Mercury - throat centre*
> *Indigo, ruled by Neptune - brow centre*
> *Violet, ruled by Uranus - crown centre*

Meditation and Channeling

HANNAH

Which is of most benefit to the Universe, to meditate on one particular focus or as a whole, given the many devastating issues worldwide. Please could you give us some direction on the most needed?

AT-HLAN

When you are meditating in your own place, by yourself, you put yourself at the centre of that meditation and you focus upon, as far as your knowledge has evolved, the information you have received. You will find for yourself which is the most important focus for you at this stage of your development. You see, one person would sit and focus on the plight of the dolphin, another upon refugees and the innocent spirit beings in the Bosnian war, another may meditate upon the pollution of the planet, another may link in with spirit friends, another may work on a cosmic level. You cannot work beyond that which you have neither overt or esoteric knowledge about. Sometimes your meditation will bring these two into balance, you may find your past knowledge and future knowledge will play a part in your own focus of meditation. So you focus in upon that which you have knowledge for and which is positive and meaningful for you.

KERRY-ANNE

This question is about the art of meditation. I can meditate for 30 minutes and not see a thing, then I start thinking that it is a waste of time and I know if I talk to a handful of people they say the same. So, does it actually benefit us meditating and not receiving anything?

AT-HLAN

It depends of course upon the focus, the point of your meditation. You can meditate for many different reasons; it is interesting that my channel has found this way of meditating, not only for himself and others in your circle, but for you, which is why he has made the tape. But the point and the focus of your meditation is important for you may sit quietly and use 20-30 minutes to send out your thoughts for others on the earth plane, you may send out your links with the spirit world or cosmic world. You may sit and meditate for a particular person to ease their pain and suffering. So, I think the most important thing for you is to work with the logical side of your brain and ask yourself why you are sitting. You see you have two guides with you when you sit in meditation who will help you. You will still have this little problem about whether it is Truth or whether it is fantasy, is it real or is it illusion. It is real, we are telling you that it is real, that you have potential there, that when you have blankness in front of you it is only because you have not tuned in to both the right level of communication and you have not focused on the reason for sitting. Does that make sense to you?

KERRY-ANNE
Yes it does, thank you At-Hlan.

MICHAEL
Is channeling the best way to receive the teachings?

AT-HLAN
Not necessarily, because we all sound a different note, we all work on slightly different vibrations and so what might be an excellent way forward along the pathway for one person, for an individual might be totally destructive for another person. This is why you have people who have dabbled as it were, who have lost their mind because they have been working in a pathway and under conditions that is totally wrong for them.

They have been open to adverse forces or they have tried to absorb energies for which they are not fit, for which they have not developed the way, the modes, the means, the structures, the network that allows them to use that energy in a positive way. The answer to your question is that each person must develop at their own stage of experience. If they have the time and the patience and start at the base and gradually acquire that which is relevant for them which they will do from meditation and other pathways then they will find the right way for them. I would not be here with my Guide Rohann to empower other people along the pathways of channeling if it were not right proper and truthful.

Indeed you will find that those who come to such Circles will be switched off if they are not at the right level. I do not put that in a hierarchical way as you know from your readings; many different people work in so many different way on this planet. This is not true of any other planet by the way and so there are many ways to universal love and universal truth.

KERRY
I would like to know how important channeling is in the work ahead?

AT-HLAN
At the present time on the earth plane, if channeling is done in the right way it is the most important work to be done on the earth plane. For as we have said before, it does not only effect the evolution, the soul evolution of mankind, the environment of Lady Earth, but it also sends out to those on a cosmic level, to those who would come in and help at this difficult time, this time of your materialisation, and so these circles become Beacons of Light. I know it is easy to say, time and time again that this is so, but unless you feel that truth within yourself then you will move to a different vibration. You yourself at the moment can feel the fineness of the vibration and the difference between what you have found in this circle and the other circle in which you have sat, is this not so?

I AM THAT I AM!

HANNAH
Could you clarify the difference between illusion and reality. What we see with our physical eyes and what we see with our spiritual beings?

AT-HLAN
I doubt it! I will attempt to!
Illusion is that which is constructed by the individual for a variety of reasons, psychologically very often to do with needs, sometimes emotional needs, sometimes emotional mental imbalance. Sometimes a way of escape, sometimes dictated by drug and alchohol abuse and so on which brings about illusion and fantasy and it is a self-made trap, it is a self-made picture which will sometimes use the senses, the nervous system. It is a cul-de-sac in which the person will learn nothing; it does not have a communication system. Only use the self with the self when you are working in the spiritual and cosmic planes - this is a reality using part of your brain and your mind and your communication system that is extrovert rather than introvert, that is probably the basic difference. Extrovert beings make links with other beings from different levels and in doing so using your more sensitive and refined thought processes, methods and means of communication.

It is developing your mind, it is making links through going through into the space time continuum throwing away that which binds you, that which holds you to the earth, that which traps you. When you have made these links then you can no longer be earth bound. Under such conditions, once your spirit is released from your body at the time in which you call death, then it can never be earth bound for you have already made links with your past, your present and your future and have come to the realisation that all are bound together so your soul is free to travel. Maybe free to travel for a while to the spiritual domain to re-establish yourself to harmonise with other influences.

For the highly developed soul to work at whatever level seems to be appropriate to your development and for taking on responsibilites at different levels and different locations. It will be surprising how at ease many of you will be in a very short time with beings from different planets. For you will sense them differently at that level. You will have a realisation that all parts of the universe are interlinked and that you may travel to different parts millions and millions of light years away in as you say a twinkling of an eye. This is not an illusion this is a fact, it is experience. The more experience you allow yourselves upon the earth plane the more realities pile up one upon the other and though it maybe against this or that teaching, this or that dogma or credalism you will know in your heart or in your mind that this is not an illusion but a fact.

HANNAH

Is it more beneficial to live in the here and now and to what extent are our future pathways effected by our past and our present?

AT-HLAN

Consider this, what is living in the here and now? We all have experiences in this life and past lives and in a sense in our future lives. By that I mean that those who have reincarnated at different times; that extensive knowledge is there for us to rediscover, to tune into and so living here and now is also living in the past and the future. However, it is possible to dwell upon the negative aspects and only experience those thought forms that are in a multitude around the earth plane and for that negativity to change the future. Remember, there is more than one future but on the other hand there is no future and past. We have our choices to make, do we not, based upon these influences, what experiences we wish to express in the future, and we have a multitude of experiences on which to draw. We shape our own future by our thoughts and actions we express at this moment in time and we reject from choice those we wish to nullify. This is a part of your own experience on the earth plane. It is possible for you to have lead a very negative past life and for much good to have come from that from other people, it may have been a learning lesson for them and in your learning experiences, before the next incarnation, you may have been able to put your experience into perspective. So all is not as it seems to be, if you see what I mean.

HANNAH

Our mission then is to try to be the living temples of the Holy Spirit to continue our spiritual initiation and to be of service to others.

AT-HLAN

Always Lady Hannah you have the freedom of choice and the very way you express things is beautiful, but always we work with people who are grounded, who are aware of their responsibilities upon the Earth Plane. There are those who have the capacity and the innate ability on the pathway which we attempt to lead you. Not so much to lead you but to counsel you, to ask you to test the pathway, ask you to listen to see if it feels right. We bring to this circle people who have had the ability and we ask them to become invigorated and motivated towards having the patience to sit, to listen and to tune in to these various planes of existence and experience, so that when they are committed in this way they pass on information at different levels some of which they understand and some of which they will not understand.

Always there are the ignorant, always there are the adverse forces and you will have your pauses, your time when you think all is not worthwhile. Also you will have the great joy of knowing the Truth, of knowing your past, present and your future all as one. You understand the oneness of being and this is a reward that we bring to you because we know of the difficulties of the existence upon the Earth plane, of the worries, of the uncertainties, the influences which are brought which are unpleasant experiences. As you progress, as you become one with The Oneness ,then this will be your reward, to be able to say, "I AM THAT I AM".

A particular future cannot be specified for, depending upon our choices, there will be alternative outcomes and so we build the future by the conditions we inspire, by the thoughts we send out and by the bridges we build between ourselves upon the Earth and those beings who would support us, from different planes, in an atmosphere of enlightenment. All we can say is that eventually we will evolve to higher levels of understanding in different bodies, under the guidance of The Great Mind.

Chapter 4   *Reincarnation*

The Evolutionary Cycle

PATSY

My question is about our evolution in terms of spirit. There are obviously more people on the earth now than at the beginning of the time so where has the balance come from?

AT-HLAN

I am just tuning in with other beings here. You know it has been said that if you compressed a person into their actual spiritual spark, the smallest atom, then all of mankind could be contained in a fairly small bottle. You see, before the earth, Gaia Tellus, was formed it was formed for a purpose, it was formed by who you refer to as your Spiritual Creator. The Creator passed on the intelligence of that network (that is the centre of all) to other beings who helped form the shape of Gaia Tellus and help bring it to the right mixture of what you call earth, water, elements and what you call spiritual beings upon it.

Before the animal kingdom - was man; before the first amoeba - was man, for man was created in God's image. But, the scientist will not have tangible evidence or proof of this, for it was in spirit form, for, as I would prefer to say, it was upon the earth plane, upon somewhat different dimensions so it would appear to your eyes to be invisible, do you see? First there was one influence, then a second influence, then a third influence over a period of millions of years and from other intelligences was formed plant life, early forms of life and an evolutionary cycle or chain was put into effect to use the environment for maximum benefit. For indeed one of the links in this chain became a form of man.

However, this form of man was not creative enough, you would say - too much left hand brain - no you would not, I correct myself there. Forget 'left hand brain' I am corrected by one of those beings who was first here*. Right - the brain system that controls the motory system and some sensitivity was in place but not the creation and so was evolved the creation part of the brain and another part that brought about logic, that was the left part smaller than you have today. They became what you would call the Black Race. But at the same time it was felt that this was not sufficient to maximise the use of such a beautiful environment, a paradise and so other beings come to bring about a diversity in man as much as there was a diversity in animal. And so you see there is a great diversity of those you call human beings here.

This of course is linked to why there are so many different choices to be made and why there are so may conflicts brought about because of those choices. For the original choices became, it is easy to say, perverted, but 'out of balance' is more correct, and there was a two-way relationship between the beings that you call mankind and the environment. Power became important rather than creation, and the enjoyment and the furtherance of the spread of God's love on the Earth plane. I will speak further upon this at a later date.

*At-Hlan is obviously conferring here and is informed that he may not be focussing upon the information clearly enough.

The Seven Root Races

HANNAH

During our last session the energy became low and you did say that we could come back to the question of the five root races. I asked a question about the different races.

AT-HLAN

You see each of the root races had information concerning future present development and this was supposed to be spread across this tiny planet, but what happened is they kept the information to themselves and created envy jealousy, conflict and so in the early stages tribes and cultures instead of spreading the light saved that truth for themselves and built idols and gods and praised it, instead of spreading it and so the network of communication became sterile, became destructive - do you understand so far?

HANNAH

Yes - because I myself have an Indian Father and an English mother and as a youngster was made to feel inadequate.

AT-HLAN

Yes - this frequently happens where there are cultural differences but you will notice for example that my channel Rohann has done quite a correct (tell him) reading for the Lady Mima and she is Spanish and he is Indian and so we are finding that there will be a lot more cross cultural mixes so that you can get nearer the truth, so that you may retreat from bias doctrine, ignorance, so that as you progress you will find that there will be a lot more mixes of the races . Genetically those that retreat into dogma, into what you would call ultranationalism particularly, become weaker and those who mix will become more liberal in their views and will get closer to the truth and genetically will grow stronger.

Darwin would be interested in such a theory, or should I say 'such a fact'. So somewhere down the line, as these ignorances are man made, as we become more spritually progressed, hopefully those fears and ignorances will be dispelled. It will be dissipated, but only by those who truly have knowledge and I would underline that there are people who would say that they are spiritual and that they have that knowledge and then they will make statements to do with racism or to do with prejudices of some sort or another which disproves the fact that they are spiritually advanced in any way, and they have taken a little knowledge and have spread it very thinly and very often have a diverse effect on other people.

HANNAH

Regarding the Black Race, is their purpose and evolution purely physical or spiritual therefore meaning that the Black race can only incarnate as the black race to fulfil their purpose for being here?

AT-HLAN

Well then you must question yourself about any being being here. What is the purpose. Being here means that you all have a place in the evolution, not just of mankind, but of the planets and of other beings, the animal, vegetable and so on. Positive influence brings all life forces forward. The Black Race..I have many people here telling me to keep this as simple as possible.. of course their part in evolution IS their part in evolution. They have the soul and the spirit the same, or similar to ,other races upon the Earth plane. Here we talk about the five root races of different colours and somewhat different forms. They have reached the stage where they are· very adaptable. In fact, because of their background very often they have teachings as all different races have to offer to other races. If we sat down on the spiritual level, you will find that all races have complimentary teachings that will help the total progress of mankind.

KERRY

Going back to the question about the Black Race, I have read or heard that they evolved from the Earth, whereas the majority of the White Race were actually incarnated from the different planets, hence the different bone structures. Can you shed any light on this please?

AT-HLAN

Well, indeed I can. Although it is not simple, the Black race were the first race to evolve upon the Earth plane. There is no evolutionary cycle that starts without the influence from the Great Mind of the Spiritual Creator by various ways and means. If we take the evolutionary cycle of planetary life, we may start from the stones, to the vegetable, to the mineral, to the animal, to mankind and so on. They have all evolved in their own way. Mankind has been given a spiritual influence from the Great Being, the Great Mind. From the Black Race came Anthropoid and so on. You may trace them back fifteen million years to the start of the evolutionary cycle of the Black Race. It is from this race that Anthropoids have come. It would be impossible spiritually and genetically for the apes to produce mankind. It would not be possible, it is against Universal Law and against the wishes of the Divine Creator and the Mind called God. At a later stage there were also beings created from the messengers of God at different areas of the Earth plane. It was found that the evolutionary status of the Black beings had been slowed down and developed sideways, a sideways move rather than a forward move. I will not go into detail at the moment but there was a slowing of forward progress.

Other beings were sent, other angels, other cosmic beings, but all from the influence of one Creator. So you have what you would call five different root races at the moment upon the Earth plane. These were created so that they could bring the different knowledge and wisdom to this important planet. The inter-relationship of ideas would develop more quickly and therefore the planetary, the cosmic system in this area would be truly creative and would shine forth a divine light. As you know, it has not happened as quickly as we have hoped because of negative influences that have been created within the cycle of mankind for power, greed and envy. This was the choice of mankind, for you were given an array of emotions to help with your progression. Some of these emotions became negative and misused rather than positive. There is still the positive influence, this planet is more protected than many, for it is important for the evolutionary cycle of this Universe.

HANNAH
Referring to the five root races, where the races have interbred, mixed was this against natural laws or will there be another race?

AT-HLAN
Yes indeed, there will be two more races which you will call the seven root races, at this stage of evolution. The influences were there, the five root races were created to produce the influences that would help each of those races. It

is not against Divine Law to do this, that mankind could be of different features, different lineage, different genealogy, would interbreed, as it were. That is not breaking divine law. Mankind must choose his own pathway to the way forward. There is no law that says you cannot be red, white, black, and so on. It is important that Love is involved in the cross fertilisation of souls. Maybe it is important in your evolution that the barriers between the different creeds and religions which have grown up, the differences in root races be broken down in such a manner that although there has been dis-information to say that there should always be separate progress by these peoples, this is not true.

Indeed, we have found during various sessions (some recorded) because of the continuing animosity, hatred and devisiveness brought about by differing religions, politics and cultures, hat energy is being withdrawn from orthodox religions, for example and individuals and groups who work for the light with commitment to truth in an open-minded way, are being empowered to see 'the way, the path and the light', and are passing on information to encourage others to take charge of their own lives.

The original plan was for different root races (basically black, brown, yellow, red, white) to offer to each other their skills and gifts and so a cross-fertilisation of ideas would assist and accelerate the soul growth of mankind. In the event, as we have experienced, races have largely tried to supress each other and, by domination, have prised away gifts (often lost in the process) and attempted to impose their own 'alien' culture.

If the plan had been successful then we (all of us) would have recognised each other as brothers and sisters from the same spiritual source. This is something that many seem to have achieved at a soul level, affirming that in previous incarnations they were Egyptian, Greek, North American Indian and so on - the same soul experiencing different cultures. This has not, until recently, had a positive effect upon relationships between peoples from a different cultural heritage, and so what is beginning to occur is a literal physical cross-fertilisation. hundreds of thousands of people from different persuasions, cultures and colours are inter-marrying and successfully producing intelligent 'balanced' human beings.

When asked by a racist what I thought was the answer to keeping out 'coloured' immigrants, I replied "It would be an excellent plan if all the people on the earth were coloured green with blue stripes and all worshipped the God of love". There was an abrupt end to the conversation but it would appear that At-Hlan and the master initiates have had similar thoughts!

HANNAH

Greetings At-Hlan. Please could you give us some more information on the other two root races. Will they come from another part of the Universe or will they develop on this planet?

AT-HLAN

Basically they will develop in what was called the 'New Worlds' in the North American continent and in Australia. These are new people with many mixtures of races. Unbeknown to them there will be planetary influences that will bring to bear their wisdom and knowledge. As you know in North America with these new races there are still many differences of opinion between the different colours and races. There will be, as it were, a force that many will recognise because so many people now feel the planetary influences. You will find in the North American continent that there are more people communicating and channeling information from various planetary influences at the moment than in any other place.

There will be influences felt very strongly from the planet Vega, that my channel; Rohann has had much to do with, and that will be the next planetary influence. Also there will be an influence from Aldebaran, which I have already mentioned. So you will not suddenly perceive little extra-terrestrial walking around in the North American continent. That influence will be felt and that place will take off in a certain direction to bring lightness. It is the older places of communication of deeper teachings that will also be linked in from India, Britain and from other countries that will be able to help and support that influence. Those who have reached a good stage of development, as has always been, will help with the dissemination of knowledge, so that there will be more control and there will be people , as it were, to sort the wheat from the chaff. We must always remember that there are alternative or negative influences as well as the pure truth

ANNE

I know quite a lot about the spiritual but I know a limited amount about the Cosmic force. Is it actually the higher realms of the spiritual world or is it an entirely different thing?

AT-HLAN

Always the simplest questions are the most complicated! When your earthly flesh passes away you will ascend to what is called the spiritual realms. The spiritual Universe is a place where you will review your life, your influences all based upon what you have done with your love, how you have shared and cared. The most humble beggar may become the greatest spirit and the richest person the most humble and disdainful spirit. You have all that to look forward to, so there is a time of equilibrium. It is not in time but in thought experience and is quite difficult to explain, for as you have had perceptions of, sometimes you can compact a whole life time, as you have done Lady Anne, within five minutes you have gone through a whole lifetime have you not? You have compacted ideas, you have travelled emotionally in many directions which is quite frustrating and disorientating for you.

Time is of little significance in the spiritual realms. There are other realms of existence in the spiritual world for those who need it, finer bodies to inherit. You have seven bodies with you at the moment and so you may leave one and inherit the other to experience a finer vibration. You may then come back for another life to do something with another life, to do something which was left undone. Perhaps it may have been decided by you and by others that you need new experiences to progress further.

There are no general rules, you see the trouble with mediumship, as my channel will no doubt remind you, is that it is sometimes impossible to link with someone who has passed to the spirit realms very quickly. The have found that they have gone home to one of the stars that influenced this planet, such as Vega, Rigel or Capella and so on. All of these form part of a network of your experiences and as you travel along that pathway your experience becomes wider and wider. The Truths that you understand have wider implication and you take on more responsibilities to advance further. It maybe that you reach a certain level in the spiritual plane and you wish to come back to help guide someone that the Lady Patsy might draw for you, an advanced being who has incarnated many times but also has a higher spiritual experience as well.

Reincarnation and Soul Evolution

HANNAH

Obviously there is a difference between the term 'group soul' and 'separate soul' Could you please give us your explanation?

AT-HLAN

You see, as an individual soul you have freedom of choice within the Universal Plan upon this particular planet, this tiny speck of dust. That choice inevitably involves other people, other entities, other souls. Over a period of time there are links made with other souls who may well have started at the same level upon the same vibration. So, links are made. These links are not necessarily sustained at the same time for all of these spiritual beings there. For one, they may have to incarnate for many times. For another, they may take a trip to another part of the Cosmos to bring back that knowledge. So in the overall Plan that group soul will grow and we would hope that this knowledge will be passed to larger groups of people so that many will evolve along certain lines and be aware of their past, present and future. This does not always work of course, for sometimes the group soul progresses, sometimes it is weakened. There is frustration or the wrong pathway has been adhered to, bringing in dogma, doctrinaire and belief systems so that a group soul may have to undergo many changes and splits and join another group of souls with which it has closer ties along the evolutionary pathway. Those who have lost their way will return at a different time and a different place. So there you have it in a complicated nutshell!

It is an interesting session this, for we have gone beyond the bounds of information that has been allowed to be given before and certainly of what you will have remembered here any of you, including our channel, for these other entities, these other beings, are tuning in more and more to help me to help you.

In answer to some of the 'early' questions asked by members of the group, At-Hlan only hinted at some of the future developments and possibilities but, as time passed and he became more confident in our commitment then he gave more detailed answers, obviously in consultation with other beings. All the answers to all the questions ever thought are extant in the plane of universal consciousness, but whether the plane and time are right seems to be another matter. I suppose this is a question of 'higher' responsibility inasmuch as too much information given at the wrong time may lead to confusion and dismay rather than assisting with our pathways of progression. Bearing in mind it is always our choice as to what we accept then we need to receive information that we can cope with and find helpful at a particular stage.

KERRY

I heard it said that progression is open to every human soul, so how is it that some people can incarnate time after time and do not seem to progress?

AT-HLAN

You see it depends what we mean by progression. For one person progression may mean being a capable, caring responsible parent capable of encouraging, counselling offspring so that tomorrow's world, as it were, becomes a better place, working at a higher vibration. For another person it may be that you aspire to become a higher form of energy such as a Master or an Avatar, because you have choice. It is true that in reincarnation you are offered more positivity, what you would call positive Karma, than the last incarnation. But it is not necessarily used to it's maximum potential, it is not necessarily used beneficially, it can be changed to a negative force and because you have choice, some of those beings will insist that they swill around in the most bestial forms of animalistic incarnations and become very strong negative influences upon all those around them.

You have choice, but it is not always used correctly. So those people do not progress. Although you are given many times to incarnate upon the Earth plane, if the choice is rejected in a positive manner time after time after time, you will find that although sections of mankind and their souls will aspire, will evolve, will take on greater responsibility, others will not and so they are left behind. They will have to learn their lessons over again in a different life form in its widest sense (this is where Buddhists have their ideas of reincarnating as a worm, toad or cow). But this happens to those souls who have rejected God's love. When you think about it it is only logical.

KERRY

You get many people who come back and cause so much mayhem and misery to fellow mankind, what happens to them when they pass over?

AT-HLAN

There are many answers to this question, for on the Spirit plane these negative people - and a gentleman commonly known as Hitler, although that is not his name, is quoted very often - has to go to the darker realms of spirit - it is a fallacy to say 'the earth plane' it is the darker realms of spirit that a person has built for himself, - surrounded by the atmosphere and environment of that person. They have to ask themselves what they have done with their lives and sometimes they will swill around quite enjoying that negativity until they get bored, until they realise that they are not progressing, until they realise that they need to progress. Then a kindly, guiding light is sent to them which sometimes they reject, when they reach that time when they accept then they are raised higher to that degree of light that they can see themselves and the environment they have created then they will wish to ask for forgiveness, they will wish for God's Love. This will take many thousands of years and at that end of that time they may not necessarily return to an incarnation upon this planet but on another planet. Have I begun to answer your question?

Again, from further conversations we have found reference to re-incarnation, not as a worm, but as a primitive soul on a planet in a different evolutionary time-scale. A kind of 'back to square one' situation in which the 'unlearned' soul has to learn lessons under more difficult conditions in which soul evolution is even slower than on earth, but perhaps surer!

It seems that the 'human soul', if we may refer to it as such, does not necessarily only progress through the spiritual realms in an ever more rarified state of existence, but may incarnate on another solar planet or a planetary system light years away. This will depend upon several factors including what we need to learn to expand soul-growth or knowledge, which star-path influences us - indeed many are beginning to feel or 'know' that they may have begun life upon, say, Vega or Sirius - and where we are in our own understanding of our own development.

All this relates to experiences undertaken in past lives and to which level we have aspired in terms of sacrifice and commitment to others upon the earth and cosmic planes. When the soul, or 'spark of God" has developed to the level when it can assess itself, (through mind and brain) often through a medum or channel, then information may be received cocerning the way forward, under universal law, in making stronger links with the network propagated by the Great Mind.

We are cosmic beings (after all God is the cosmic force that activates us) who are responsible for the evolution of our own souls, including the group soul of mankind, and play an important part of the evolution of the solar planetary system. We have a relationship with many star systems for we are an integral part of them as they are of us.

Karma and Karmic Balance

KERRY

What I would like to know is, because of the way everything is changing, people are becoming more aware of the cosmic influences, what is going to happen to those who refuse to believe it, they are not just going to accept it. So, you have got those who are progressing and those who are standing still.?

AT-HLAN

You must remember that we are all interlinked, and those who progress are helping the progression of others, whether they understand that at that level or not. Before, you see, many of those people that I would have mentioned from all over the world who have suddenly taken a different path, much to their own surprise, do not necessarily believe in cosmic influences or the world of spirit, but they are still influenced unconsciously through the thought you send out. So they do not have to know, they do not have to understand, they merely act upon the wavelength that guides and councils them in the direction of peace and harmony. Of course there are those who will always be a negative influence who refuse to involve themselves in the evolution of the soul, and have become earth bound or trapped and incarnate again and again making the same mistakes. Eventually in hundreds and thousands of years time when you have evolved to the high degree of grace they would be returned, ashes to ashes, dust to dust, to start their cycle of evolution once more.

PATSY

You have said that some souls with great negativity are sometimes re-incarnated not on this planet but on another. Is this because they would more easily make the transition to a more positive life without the free choice that they have on this planet?

AT-HLAN

You see there are different ways of going about this, as I mentioned before it is not as straightforward as people imagine. If there has been a group soul, I will talk in terms of soul groups, for you see there may be a point of focus around what you may call a negative individual because of their darkness over an area of the Earth plane, but at the same time there will be many links of other negative individuals who are sparked into operating the negative pathway. So, it is more of a group soul activity, although the focus may be around one or two individuals. It may be that these spirit entities have sometimes erred along the wrong pathway in trying to get to the correct pathway, it is not always that they seek to become destructive, but have become destructive at a level they are not aware of. So instead of being part of what you would normally think of as spiritual progression they might well be contacted to be taken to another part of the Cosmos under the guidance of entities who you call extra-terrestrials, to learn a particular pathway. When they re-emerge, re-incarnate upon the Earth plane, they are more aware of the positivity they are able to offer than the negativity. Some of them have come from an area where their vibration may be positive, but when they come here they try the same vibration and it does not work because of the different conditions. This leads to frustration and the negative pathway.

You see, all this information breaks down the stereotype thoughts, for example of your many religions and creeds that have risen upon the Earth plane, that are sometimes from the best, as far as they are concerned, from the highest point of view. They think that they are progressing but they have cast off the thoughts and the memories that they have had of these past experiences. Therefore they have, as it were, gone along a certain limb of a tree and perhaps too late, find that the limb has withered and they have moved away from the mainstream of the pathway of Cosmic Being and of Universal consciousness.

MARTIN
I have recently read that some souls are in a permanent cycle of reincarnation on earth and are not willing to fully appraise their position and look at their incarnations elsewhere. What can you say on this?

AT-HLAN
I am not sure that I understand the question my brother, but you see I will expand upon what I consider your meaning to be. Many souls on the earth plane go through many thousands of years and experience finer and finer spiritual realms and sometimes they choose to work upon other planetary systems and sometimes in a different universe for there are more universes than the ones that you actually see materially from this earth plane. There are other spiritual entities that remain trapped on the lower spiritual realms and can reincarnate without

having any progression so that they bring back negative influences with them to the earth plane. Some of them, as you have read and have sensed, remain in the lower realms as a negative influence for many many years if not thousands of years. Other souls may have in the past had their experiences upon other cosmological points and then return to the earth plane.

At the same time there are beings from other planets who have incarnated upon the earth plane. This is a fascinating subject and one that has been very thought provoking by members of the human race who have not had the information to hand. This is because they have not been able to meditate and reveal the knowledge that is within and also, if they wish project, as that feeds our energy, as extra information is given to them as this evening some of you have been taken to past lives to experience that because you wish to project that information on the ether, you might say. It is because we wish you to learn more about the past and the future that this information is given to you so freely.

MARTIN

Does it mean that someone could sacrifice their existence in this incarnation for the benefit of others and in that incarnation appear very negative and building up a lot of karma?

AT-HLAN

Yes, what is sacrifice? This is a very interesting word you see. Some souls, some sparks of the great creator may give the illusion that they have made sacrifice on behalf of other people and it may appear to those other people who are feeling sorrow or remorse that this was a good life. But what have they learnt, how are they left, their own progression has stultified, it has turned from joy to sadness. This is how some of your Masters have lead their lives. It is more self-aggrandisement, it is sometimes even to appear a grand and joyful soul and this is a mask which covers an incarnation where an entity is very negative and has spread despair instead of upliftment. So your actions must match your words and your words must reveal the Truth and when this is revealed then you will draw to you those who become uplifted. There are those who have apparently lead a negative life, you read in your bible of the lady who was saved by the Jesus figure, through the Christ light, who was about to be stoned to death and she saw no evil in the people who surrounded her, this is a parable of many different meanings.

The Cycle of Reincarnation

AT-HLAN

We have been doing 'past life '(or regression) work for three or four people during the last week or so and this has been very therapeutic for those concerned, for it unblocks sometimes a past life from a trauma and takes away a shadow from the aura that you may have brought with you into the present and so then progression is then allowed to be made. But, the person doing this work has to be very sensitive, needing great counselling skills for this to be positive rather than negative. It is something that the psychiatrist and psychologist know very little about, they beat about the bush with their trivial and superficial work, whereas the real work very often is what you carry in your aura and in your soul and so that emanates from past lives. So, this is a channel that has been opened up. I am telling you this for a reason that I will not explain, but there is a reason for someone to know about past lives and previous incarnations because this is the Truth, whatever has been said by churches, by dogma,by adopting their approaches the whole process of mankind's evolution and increasing soul awareness would indeed not make sense without the process of reincarnation and indeed how do I come here and how do other guides come here to you, that in itself is a reincarnation at a different level. Perhaps some of you would have some questions to do with the aura or soul awareness or incarnation for this very rich vein of thought and questioning and also of wisdom.

SYBIL

Are there people amongst us who are going to do this in the future?

AT-HLAN

This is a new channel that has been opened and certainly there will be some in this circle who will be capable of doing such work and certain rigorous procedures and training. Are there any more direct questions to do with what I have introduced into your circle for a purpose this evening.

PENNY

I would like to know, as we are now aware of spirit and we are sensitive, but I wasn't always, it has only been in the last two years that I have come to know about this, when we pass over and then reincarnate shall we reincarnate with the same stage of awareness or have we got to wait another lifetime and then gradually become aware again?

ATHLAN

When you leave this existence and you go into the spiritual universe as you call it, you take with you the experiences of this lifetime and of previous lifetimes, many of you will go into the spiritual universe to learn further because you do not stop learning, some people have a time of peace and harmony when they have to establish certain things about their own souls, depending upon what you have learned here and in the spiritual universe then you will choose a time to reincarnate. For some people this is a very quick process for they are keen to come back to teach as wise souls, to contact other people and draw them and guide them and counsel them along the pathway of light, upliftment and truth. Other people may have to stay in the grey land for a considerable amount of time until the light shines again and they are aware of the negative karma that they have done on the earth plane and even so, when they incarnate they make the same mistakes, they do not progress and so the process is repeated time and time again until the true light shines for them.

CAROL

I know if we all have our destinies to learn in this life, if we went through the process of regression would that help us with our lessons or would we still have to go through and learn them even though we could be taken back to learn them through regression?

ATHLAN

You will still have your lessons to learn, that would not be changed. But if there has been problems with your past lives then you may well learn those lessons more quickly, more accurately in a more focused way, more in control of that which confronts you of that test or that trial. You will be able to discriminate more easily, you would accelerate your learning and therefore you would be able to fit more into the earthly experience than you would have done before hand.

DEBRA

If we want to try regression here within the circle would we need that lady to come and do it, could we do it with your teachings, or is it going to take us months and months or are we going to be able to do it one evening instead of the circle.?

AT-HLAN

Well we can fulfil this part if that is what people wish. Certainly this lady that has been mentioned is a centre of Truth and integrity to do this work. But, in some ways you have already done some forms of regression, you yourself lady Debra, have undergone some form of regression. Yes, it is possible to do this for those who wish to do it, not necessarily all the different lives for this would take too long,but important lives, lives in which we can look into the aura and through the aura into the bodies, into the soul and say at this point in someones life a calamity, a shock, a taking of the wrong pathway, something that has been soul genetically imprinted, something that has been carried from the past life. We could undertake this work so when you are fit and you yourself and one or two other people in this circle also, this may be, if it goes in that direction another part of your work because it is still a truth , the light.

The term 'regression' is not strictly accurate; what was specifically understood by this is a past life reading. 'The Lady' referred to actually undertook past life regression work.

KERRY

Who decides and when is it decided when a person is right to walk along the spiritual path because the age difference varies. You have someone who might start at 22, then you have someone who might start at 60, why?

AT-HLAN

Well, that would depend very much on their past lives, on why they have chosen to incarnate into this life, what they wish to learn in this life, whether they have learnt experiences, whether they have opened up their etheric channels and for some this may start at a very early age, indeed increasingly, as you have found, there are those at a younger age who have the capacity and the experience to participate in the forming of circles such as this. This is because they have chosen to do so in a former life, they have had cosmic experience in previous lives, they are open and aware at a super-conscious level. For others they may have left the pathway and returned to it, they may have chosen to fulfil their earthly lives in different ways, simply as parents or grandparents or to attach themselves to helping in childcare, samaritans or other good causes. You see, there are many pathways to the same source are there not.?

Karma and Karmic Influences

PATSY

Is there an average number of incarnations that we go through or does it differ from person to person.?

AT-HLAN

It differs from person to person. There are still some primitive souls on the Earth plane who have incarnated very few times because from early days they were very negative. They acquired negative karma so when they went to the spirit world they spent a long period of time, perhaps 1-2,000 years trying to learn the lessons of their past lives, ready for the next life. If the lessons of the past life are very few then it will take longer to learn them for the next life. Sometimes it has been known for a spirit to leave a body and reincarnate in another body in a matter of days, this is where the Hindu's get their philosophy, but on average in a region of 170-250 years is average. New souls reincarnate more quickly than old.

LENETTE

Why would a group soul wish to come back and suffer as they have done in Rwanda. Why do root races appear to suffer in this manner, like Africans, Asians and people of the Eastern Continents?

AT-HLAN

It is part of the evolutionary process. You see, very often these people have inflicted hurts and have made war, torture and chaos, upsetting of the balance before. So, they come back as a sacrifice to empower other people, to inform them that this is not the way. The way forward is that all humanity progresses in the Light, without politics, without religion, without envy, avarice and prejudice. Although it appears at the time that these innocent people, women and children in particular suffer such tortures, in the longer term it is a teaching for the rest of humanity. Sometimes there are of course Karmic debts, karmic atonement to be made. Often there have been battles for thousands of years that re-appear because people have not yet learned their lesson as you have found in the former Yugoslavia. The Croats and the Serbs have been battling with each other over thousands of years under different names. They have not learned their lessons and that is a different matter, so there are different reasons none of which were meant to happen but because you are given freedom of choice then all these things have to be worked through.

Eventually mankind will come to a realisation of the equality of all.. Always of course there are those who refuse to learn, as you might say, lower spirits, those who refuse to learn from the actions both by themselves and by others. They will not proceed on the next evolutionary stage and will send themselves to a lower stage of existence and have to start at a lower level. This does not mean necessarily, as the Hindus describe, as a cow, or a cat or a worm, but a different place in the plane of things, a different part of the Universe, one which is not so well endowed with the Light, with the variety of life that is so prevalent upon Gaia, upon Mother Earth, but that you see is their choice.

MARY
Could you explain please how Karma works.

AT-HLAN
This is, by and large, a Buddhistic term. Your karma works in many different ways, for, as you explore your experiences from other incarnations you will have found that, sometimes, you will have taken a backwards step, you have influenced others in a negative way, you have not been sharing and caring. In other incarnations you have sacrificed yourself, you have sacrificed your own personal freedom, you have anchored yourself to a place called Truth and maybe have been tortured or attacked for this Truth. So, there is good karma and there is bad karma. We have found that in this life time, this incarnation many, due to the cosmic influences upon the earth plane are going through an accelerated balance of Karma. So you will find many upon the earth plane who require guidance and counselling along the pathway of life for they are lost souls looking for a leader, as it were, looking for the Truth and the Light.

In this lifetime many people will balance their karma, will have a positive karma to enable them to participate in the next cycle of evolution. You will find that many who come to these circles have a positive karma, so that they are easily channeling infinite love, they can look back on their lives, good, bad and indifferent, without fear. There are a few who, because they come to a circle, will balance that, for they are working for the great mind and in their lives in

Truth and commitment they bring the Light to shine for themselves and for others. So, this is another positive balance of karma. There are great Lords of karma, great initiates, who, every time you are born and reborn in the life and death cycle, you are given , no matter how badly you have lead your lives previously, you are given a little more positive karma to work with. So, this does not mean that you necessarily walk in the Light, again you may disabuse yourself of that Light and walk in the darkness for a time. But always there are opportunities for you to progress, no soul is left in the darkness forever. For, as you call them, the Grey Lands, the places where you have to face that which you have achieved or that which you have negated, in those places always there are guides of light to help you into the light, for the Great Mind works on the vibration of love and not of darkness.

CAROL
Is karma purely personal, or does it affect other people?

AT-HLAN
It is both, it works at both an individual level and at a group soul level, and what you might call a cultural or national level. If we take, for example, present day Yugoslavia, there have been battles among those fundamentaly different cultures for hundreds if not thousands of years, temporarily those differences were suppressed, in this case by a dictator whose name was Tito, but now they are released they have their full freedom of expression they go into battle once more, they have not learned their cultural or national or even group soul lesson, which is concerned with the pathway forward to peace and understanding, towards the Brotherhood of mankind. So, they involve themselves as warriors, involve others who are innocent, who sacrificed themselves in this cause, and so as a result of this those who are innocently sacrificed will find that they will progress more quickly in their next incarnation than those who are deeply aware of their own negative influence in the killing, the slaying, the torture of others, will find that they have acquired much negative karma which will take an awful long time in earthly terms to clear, to bring back the positive balance so that they may reincarnate having learned of that lesson. There is a limited duration, a limited cycle of reincarnation for these people, so that if they refuse to learn their lessons, if they use their choices negatively time and time again then they will find that incarnation occurs, perhaps not upon this planet, but in a different planetary system where they are regressed to learn from a very early stage of

being , when the soul is in a very much more primitive state, when there does not appear to be choices, but are conditioned by the environment at that place until they reach such a stage when they are able to make choices. So, always there are negative and positive influences and until such a stage is reached when that positive influence will take on a challenge at a much higher level of development. So, a new galaxy or planetary system is formed from that conflict. This is one of the reasons why I am here, is to give you knowledge, not just at an earthly or spiritual plane of existence but always to link you with the Great mind through the high spiritual beings to say time and time and time again you have a part to play in the cosmos, you are a cosmic being, and with your being there is responsibility for the evolution not only of this planetary system but certainly for this part of the galaxy, this part of the Universe. But do not feel burdened by this responsibility for there are many others that support you on all other planes of existence.

The Pathway to Future Existence

KERRY

We are all in agreement that we are striving for harmony and peace worldwide. Will there be a time when we as a human race, with the intervention of beings such as yourself, achieve a life without wars, murders and all the unpleasant happenings that we have to endure on a daily basis? And, will I be around to see it?

AT-HLAN

Well, the latter part of your question depends upon your own progression, your own pathway and choices. So, Lady Kerry-Anne, you may be around to see it, but not in this lifetime of course. The former part of your question is that it is inevitable for this is evolutionary progress. You refer to humankind, by this stage of evolution they may be unrecognisable to you in comparison to what you see as human beings at the present time of the evolutionary cycle of mankind and the planet and the Cosmos. This is also inevitable for it would be impossible to reach that higher stage of progression with the interfering factors that have surrounded you, both within and without the dense physical conditions in the body and the Earth. This is also part of the evolutionary cycle of events, so you are still really at the platform. It is rather like heating water, you have the fluid there which is at a higher level, in a sense, than the solid wood which the vessel rests on, and if you heat the water you will know that molecules rise up and become steam, a more refined level. Some of that comes back, metaphorically, to the water and it is possible through the evolutionary chain of course that the steam becomes more refined, which then becomes more refined and so on. I hope that this is not too much of a difficult way to explain.

As we have taken millions of years to reach our present stage of evolution upon this planet, re-incarnating many, many times (and for some, or many, having experienced life upon other planets) it might seem fairly obvious that it may take as long again to fulfil the full potential of our evolutionary pathway and thereby ascend to become empowered souls enabled to play a fuller part in the development of the universe as beings of light or highly evolved cosmic masters. However, as there is an acceleration in learning and perception taking place at this time due to an intensified cosmic vibration or energy force that is interpenetrating the electro-magnetic field of the earth to 'lift' the evolutionary cycle then people begin to assume that we will become angelic beings or escape from earth with the influence of cosmic beings next week, next year or, at least, in a few years time.

Not so, says At-Hlan, for we are 'at the platform' which, loosely translated, I take to mean that we are at the half-way point or stage in this evolutionary cycle and, although exciting and uplifting influences are certainly around to help those with 'eyes to see and ears to hear' it will be thousands or millions of years before we may leave the cycle to be completed upon this planet. Of course there are exceptions for, as we have always had master initiates and cosmic masters working upon the earth plane, as human beings (as well as working upon the spiritual and cosmic planes) then it may be that to assist in developing the present cycle many more 'humans' may find, as they turn to the light of unconditional love and begin to tune into universal consciousness that they have a large part to play in the process. We are involved in raising soul consciousness fairly quickly to a higher level and potentially producing many more initiates, and as they progress and guide increasing numbers along the pathway of truth (who we are and what our purpose is) so the evolutionary cycle brings in great changes to establish us as universal beings.

Against this background of logical progression it seems utterly inconceivable that some select few will be 'beamed up' to escape to some cosmic heaven, for we create our own paradise (or hell) here on earth. In part the journey towards fuller soul consciousness and awareness means that we strive to overcome the difficulties that beset us, and as individuals and with groups we work towards the emancipation and integration of all humanity. With the release of the shackles that bind -religious, ethnic, cultural and political differences - then the soul is free to express itself, to acknowledge that we are all brothers and sisters from the same spiritual source, The Great Mind, and then - perhaps as one - we may all be 'beamed up' to participate in greater responsibilities at a cosmic level.

KERRY

Why is that some people experience such wonderful phenomena, whilst others do not go beyond seeing, hearing stage, although this in itself is a wonderful gift, a lot want more evidence. What do we have to do to achieve this.

AT-HLAN

Well you see we have to go back to past lives, we have to go back to past experiences. Some have re-incarnated at a very simple level, at a very simple life, to achieve very simple things. Sometimes of course these people have had lives of ignorance and they have inflicted injuries, mental or physical upon other people. They come back to learn the simple life, they have not progressed. We must get away from the idea that all people progress at the same rate, they do not. Some people have worked very hard in their progression and have opened their lives to light. And so you find, as you have found, people who have suffered in this life and some who have suffered in past lives, still progress, are aware and sensitive of different levels of existence almost from birth, before birth as well, despite the fact that they have been born into cruel conditions or adverse conditions, perhaps for some learning they wished to learn from that. And sometimes this adds to and heightens their awareness of all the different choices, all the different emotions that are available to you.

And so, very highly evolved souls will have learned about the greatest sadness and the happiest joys of existence on the Earth Plane. It is not until the whole range, the whole plethora of these emotions have been experienced fully that you can become, for example, a Chohan, a Cosmic Master. It is not self imposed misery but part of the learning process. But we must discriminate between those and others who come back time and time again and live a life of ignorance and what you would call sin, and of hurt, pride and of envy and of sloth and so on. There are souls also who have come back under those conditions and simply feel that they enjoy these conditions and refuse to progress and of course as many of you progress to higher and higher realms these will, having been offered many opportunities, regress and go in the opposite direction until they have to start all over again and learn properly how to fulfil the potential of the divine love, the spirit or spark of God that they were given and it may well be that they do regress to a lower level than mankind and the human soul.

That will not happen until the progression of mankind has reached it's zenith and the evolution of this planetary system has been fulfilled and when many migrate at a higher level to take on more responsibility in the Cosmos, in the universe and empower progression in other parts of the Universe. So you see all is choice, all is driven and ruled by Universal Law. It is very pleasant to know that many millions of souls upon the Earth Plane at the moment are reaching great levels of awareness and are sending out and receiving love and humour and charity and so on and there is a great vibration at the moment in which many are participating, and I was looking forward with my senses to see many lifted in joy and happiness and reaching the stage of the Angels and beyond and being empowered to work in other systems and beyond where there are souls who need to be pushed forward in their evolutionary days to start the motivation of new planetary systems. This will generate life upon other planets and they will be able to communicate with the star systems and lend their power and energy to create new life because this is the future of a very evolved soul.

HANNAH
I have heard of the state of Devechan, is that a state of Utopia?

AT-HLAN
Devechan is used as a term of at-one-ment with the Light, at-one-ment with the Spiritual Source. This indeed takes rather a long time, millions of years. You see all those progressed from the state where they are closer to what is also called the 'Elysian Fields', the drawing close to the 'Mind of Minds', then you will have a choice either to return to the source of life or to continue the responsibility of the way at a cosmic level. At this cosmic level there are many experiences to be had and there a many battles to be fought, there are cosmic oceans to plumb, to sound out, to help with the progress from the most minute cell to those who have evolved quite highly but have left the path and brought about consternation to the maker. So there are a lot of various areas of work in which to become involved. Once you are part of this cycle there are different ways in which you may operate in harmony with others who have aspired, who have evolved to the same degree for this work. You may operate as an enormous power, as a God as it were, as a God on your own, as a God who operates with other Gods to influence cosmic wavelengths, or areas of influence. You may return to the source to increase the great progression of all things across time and space, always there are choices.

Chapter 5   *The White Brotherhood*

How and Why the brotherhood Exists

PATSY
Could you tell us about the entities that are with you, how many there are and who they are please?

AT-HLAN
I am in communication with the White Brotherhood. This means to say that I am empowered and enabled through their good graces, for they work as a catalyst would work. They are enablers, what you would call in modern jargon, facilitators. So, although they do not actively participate themselves they are allowed to open channels of communication wherever it is necessary under certain circumstances. There are also other Cosmic Beings who are higher spiritual beings with whom we have a communication. Therefore, it is possible to make links telepathically, telepathic links with beings far across the Universe, for there are considerable Universes that exist in different time and space. So there is a whole network of communication with which, for the most part, I am empowered to communicate. Certainly, because we have met under these circumstances and conditions it is possible to make links for you and with you to bring in a very wide realm or area of knowledge, to tune into that which is called Universal Consciousness and to answer your questions in some detail. However, as we have found last week, a simple question may lead to many, many answers. For there are so many different beings who would wish to communicate and bring in their area of knowledge so that a simple question may be answered sometimes on too many different levels, for we need to focus in on a particular aspect to that question. You see the people from Altair, Vega, from Polaris and way into the distance as far as you are concerned, will come in to help. The distance is nothing as far as we are concerned for it is immediate.

It may come as rather a shock that the White brotherhood are Extra-terrestrial influences, as explained in chapter one, who were 'here' before the earth was formed, who were influences in the formation of this planet and perhaps the solar planetary system. Although there have been many references to them it has not been specific, as documented in this chapter, and many civilisations have 'seen' them in a different way.. For example, the early North American Indians experienced them as tall figures wearing white feathered head-dresses down to the ground. Surely, because we 'see' them, at least, more nearly as they are, as cosmic beings, then this has something to say concerning both our level of development and the cosmic energies that influence our planetary system at this moment in time.

94

KERRY
Greetings to you At-Hlan. We would like to know who are the White Brotherhood and what part do they play in our progression.

AT-HLAN
The White Brotherhood have been in existence for eons and eons of time. As each planet in the system evolves the White Brotherhood have responsibilities for each of the planets. In a way they are almost timeless beings. By your standards they would be tens of millions of years old. With reference to your planet Earth they were part of the influence of the infra-structure through the Great Spirit, that brought about this planet into being. They have more direct influences in the past that dates back to legend and mythology. Although they were not present in the material sense, they brought their Cosmic influences to bear on various aspects of mankind. You have reached, in your evolution in this span of time, a place where they may come to visit you, as they have done in your circles, and indeed they are present at the moment. They take a great interest in these matters, they will observe and help to focus the light, the communication systems, colour and all these different wave lengths, but they will not participate themselves actively but they will send telepathic messages or produce images for your brain to receive.

Although they are attracted to the light they communicate with other beings who may then relate and become part of that communication network. They are very high beings, who come from a planet or a system which in fact has now gone out of existence. As far as this present state of awareness is concerned they are so evolved they have transferred to a different system, a different plane which would be invisible to the scientists on this planet, from what you may call a parallel universe. They have the ability to almost instantaneously travel through what is called time and space. They alter the vibration so that with a few people you will find that there is an image and that they appear, as I have said, to be timeless. They are called the White Brotherhood for there are a number of them allocated in this area of the Universe. They form a Brotherhood when the communication system appears by your eyes to appear a pure white light. They also may appear simultaneously at different places upon the Earth Plane. They also have the ability to become multi-dimensional. I will pause there for you to consider that and to wait for another question, if that is sufficient for the time being.

HANNAH

Have they always been closer to God, like Angelic Beings?

AT-HLAN

They were a civilisation before this Universe was being developed. They are a product of the environment carrying out the work of the Great Spirit, so in terms of time, they would be very early on in the development of this planet . They related to the early stars that were formed when,as is said, God drew himself into himself and threw himself across the Universe. What your scientists have not yet recognised is that this is only one of the Universes that was created by the Great Mind.

PATSY

Have they ever lived materially on Earth or have they just been in Spirit?

AT-HLAN

No, they have never lived materially on Earth for it would be impossible. They have retained their form and their abilities for, as far as I have said, eons and eons of time. They would not wish or be enabled to incarnate upon the Earth Plane, it would be an impossibility. It is not , you see, possible for beings to incarnate upon the Earth Plane only those who are enabled to do so for the progression of this planet,and they come merely from a few hundred light years away. These people, if you will understand me, come millions of light years away, so that their abilities are great. They are not empowered to incarnate, indeed they work at such a high level, a sophisticated level, that if they were to try it would be disastrous for the power that they carry within them. Firstly, they would not be in tune with the 'fleshly' person upon the Earth Plane, and secondly they might cause rather an explosion!

The Work of the Brotherhood

PATSY
So all their progression has been done in another Universe or elsewhere in the Universe. So have they progressed to the White Brotherhood.?

AT-HLAN
Well, this is an interesting question because you see there is not always what you would call natural progression. These highly able people are, if you like, higher than the highest Chohan*. They have acquired abilities from several Universes not just one Universe. So if you had a pyramid with the highest Avatar in your dimension at the top then you would have to create several other pyramids before you got to the White Brotherhood. In this particular case they were formed very early to help with further development. Given this knowledge and ability without having to go through what you would call the painful process of evolution. To put it in a nutshell, they did not need to progress from time to time, from planet to planet, but they are 'enablers' for others to participate in this.

*Chohan - Master Initiate at a cosmic level of existence.

SUSAN
Are we destined to progress as far as the Whitebrotherhood?

AT-HLAN
Well that is a matter for the individual. You see, it comes down to personal choice, and the progression that you can carry out is either to become very high in your pyramid at which time you may have the opportunity and the ability either to choose to do more basic work on another planatary system, another star system or another galaxy, or you may aspire higher back as it were towards the Great Mind. But you will never become a White Brother for they are unique, their abilities and skills are unique. You may develop at such a level that you maybe initiated into the White Brotherhood, because of your development and willingness to help; I am talking here of course of millions of years of your time. If I may talk of At-Hlan, myself objectively, I have been initiated into the White Brotherhood to help them with their work. But in a sense I am still quite a way down the pyramid with the White Brotherhood above me at the top. So they have enabled me to help with the development and the progress of that which is taking place upon the earth plane at this present time.

HANNAH
Are you saying then that perhaps the White Brotherhood have been in existence from the beginning of existence?

AT-HLAN
Very near the beginning of the formation of this particular universe. Yes indeed that is precisely what I am saying.

PATSY
Are any of our Guides and Teachers that work with us also initiated into the White Brotherhood?

AT-HLAN
No this is very unusual, this is rare, as it were. For as I have said I am the closest I can get to the super astral. The White Brotherhood are super super cosmic. This is the simplest way I can find for putting this. But they are drawn infrequently to those groups who have aspired with great commitment to tunein

to a very high frequency which is why my channel has been allowed to link in with and to take you on these short little cosmic journeys that you have experienced. From this knowledge and this understanding you have begun to realise that some of the things in which you believed are mythical or that they do not go far enough and so you have learned the greater truths of creation. It is hoped that with the circle of ten at some time to take you further towards the beginning of time. We can only do this because of our links with the White Brotherhood who are the protectors and inspirers in this direction.

For some reason At-Hlan has frequently inferred that 'the circle of ten' is the perfect number of committed people to assist with his work of writing this book. Occasionally we have achieved exactly that number but more often fewer people and sometimes more have regularly attended. Due to the ebb and flow of life a few have left to do other work while others have 'moved house' only to start a new circle, carrying their developed skills and our method of channeling with them. This is how the important information is disseminated. At this moment the circle is comprised of ten dedicated people but a smaller group of four volunteered specifically to sit with At-hlan for the purpose of asking the questions relevant to the content of this book.
Our 'little cosmic journeys' have so far allowed us visitations to the sun and moon and to planets in the systems of Sirius, Polaris, Vega, Alpha Centauri and a star system near Alcyone towards Aldebaran.

KERRY
When they come along to this kind of circle do they actually take part on the development of our progression or do they just come to over see?

AT-HLAN
In both ways; they come to over see, they come to register information about our development. The amount of information you can receive and use in a positive way, because in this way knowingly and unknowingly you link with others. You pass on information at a subconscious level, or at least, depending on the development of other people, maybe part of that information is passed on. They will all enable us in the sense that you will have had such people such as Azgar, Zargon and so on, who have visited your circle. So there will be other cosmic beings as some of you have already seen, felt, heard or sensed and so the network goes out and out and out.

So the potential for development is as infinite as you allow your mind to rid itself of hurdles or barricades or whatever. As this goes on more and more positive influences are brought to bear within the Circles and the more, good you do upon the earth plane the more you have to establish further links and increase the vibration, the positive vibration of good and such things as the ceasefire in Sarajevo come about. It is very easy for you to think that things are very negative on the earth plane, but when we consider the negative influences also that work and the trauma and issues of emotional power that is brought about by peoples upon the earth plane then you have helped to countermand this much more strongly than you have realisation of.

KERRY

Also, if they get drawn to a Circle that starts off with good intentions but somewhere along the line falls by the wayside, have they got the power and the authority to see this Circle dispersed?

AT-HLAN

You see it does not work in that way, there must first of all be a Circle who have the commitment, the energy and the purpose and increasing knowledge to reach a stage at which the White Brotherhood may visit. The stage which they would come in at would be full of love and joy and have very strong links already and such as a higher spiritual being. Now, if there were adverse influences upon this Circle or people misused the power then they would simply depart and those who are still working in the circle you would find that because they are not working any longer towards Truth the beings from whichever level that they drew to them, would be coming in at a lower vibration. And so eventually the group would self destruct, it would destroy its own being.

The White Brotherhood in the Universe

SUSAN

I cannot remember what you said before about White Brotherhood and the stars. Could you explain are they linked in some way?

AT-HLAN

The White Brotherhood maybe linked to an area of the universe where evolution and progression is not only needed but needs to be monitored. You see, if you could see through the eyes of the White Brotherhood you could practically see thorough time and space. They may travel wherever, through a star, through you, because it does not necessarily exist for them it only exists if they tune into whichever material vibration is in existence at that particular time and place. When they are drawn to work, and they are working not only upon this planet but they are working on other planets as well, to form a network of communication to help us with progress. When they are drawn to a particular time and place then they will project to that time and place and for some they will appear to have been seen and usually to be seen in an acceptable form. For here they will be seen as beings that are of the light, unthreatening, about four foot to four foot six high, to look intelligent and so on. In a different time and place they will appear differently.

PATSY

You have said that there are other Gods in the universe. Do the White Brotherhood involve themselves with those or are they just involved with our God and our progression?

AT-HLAN

It is very important for the White Brotherhood got their contact and relationship with this planet and its planetary system. It is quite high in the list of priorities. But they do have contact with other beings, what you might call higher beings, for you see you may in a way refer to each of the White Brotherhood as a God for they have more power, intelligence, gifts and skills than the peoples of the earth. They were given on a conscious level, on an intelligent level from the great God that made all and so they have the ability to contact other star systems and other beings that are working within those star systems. They are also aware that in some areas of the universe all is not goodness, pureness and light, so this has to be reported as well so that those beings who are working in that area of the cosmos may bring about harmony and balance. So, yes, the answer is yes if you like they do have contact with other Gods.

There are a number of references to 'other' and parallel universes throughout these channelings and it appears that the White brotherhood are able to 'transpose' themselves through time and space to have an influence in different dimensions and levels of experience. Whenever the group feel that 'we have had it solved' then another lesson pops up to remind us that, in the infinity of space wherever we have got to we are still only at the beginning.

PATSY
John said last week that Azgar had been given a special award to further his spiritual advancement which would give him permission to take on a more serious role. Does this mean he will lose his Fun-loving role?

AT- HLAN
No indeed. It does mean that Azgar will arrive in your circle to help in many, many ways because he brings so much love and happiness and joy with him. Those people have been an influence and joy for many, many years. For them a million years is very little time, because time and space is very different. You cannot always be at that level. Azgar has got much knowledge from *Zengali, from where he comes, and the influence of Sirius with knowledge to bring. He will still come on a love vibration and when you are low in spirits he will pick you up. He has also been given the information that he may now talk to you about, to do with the evolutionary cycle, both of his own race, his own people and what relationship that has and what influence that has been on this planet with your evolutionary cycle. So he has much to offer in his amusing way and is very much part of the development of knowledge among you all.

*We have found Zengali to be the third planet from Sirius.

Chapter 6 *Life on Earth*

Contents

The Evolution of the Earth

PATSY
Can I ask you a question that my youngest son Matthew asked me to ask you that is how old is the Earth and how long have people actually inhabited it?

AT-HLAN
I am not very good at mathematics and so I have asked for further help....Between 2.5 and 3 billion years, is the formation of the planet Earth and interestingly some of the scientists will find that some of the planets in the system are older and some younger. Venus, for example, is younger. Mankind has been in existence, we would say, about 15 million years, which again would upset scientists, but 15 million years as beings that you would recognise as beings , for you were not always in this shape. But at that time there were cosmic or spiritual influences forming and shaping mankind to be able to adapt to the environment, the gravity and the heat and the light at that time which has changed since then. So, a good round number is 15 million years and there will be evidence found, I have spoken of the future very little, but towards the end of the year 2020 there will be scientific evidence to support that which I have just stated.

At-hlan sometimes admits to the limitations of his own knowledge (which appears, anyway, to be vast) and pauses to confer with other beings. he appears to have easy and almost instant access to their communication systems. As we 'arrived' upon this planet from an external source then the soul-body had to arrive at a more recognisable form tens of thousands of years before 15 million years ago. Whether we were originally cosmic entities from other star systems, or were formed by The Great Mind directly is still a matter under discussion, but many of us in the circle have been informed of previous incarnations on other star systems in our galaxy and indeed feel attracted to particular stars. By and large the concensus is that we have progressed to this particular planet system having had extra-terrestrial experiences that have varied from person to person, soul to soul. In this sense we are a far more developed people than we give ourselves credit for, which is why we can communicate with other cosmic beings, for we have already developed and used that facility! It makes sense, doesn't it!

KERRY
The scientific 'boffins' are preaching that the Mother Earth is going to burn up

106

because of the ozone layer. I have actually argued the point with many people that because of higher influences that have 'investments' in Mother Earth that this will not be allowed to happen. Am I right or am I arguing a pointless cause.

AT-HLAN

No, of course this is an absolute nonsense to say that mankind has the power to destroy the progression of the Earth, it has many, many millions of years yet in it's progression; needless to say, Kerry-Anne, you may have to come back several times. Also, the other point is that influences are always brought to balance when the Earth Goddess asks for help, and it is given. There are cycles you see, you forget when you had things such as the Ice Ages and such, when ozone and these inert gases played a larger part than mankind has found at the moment. They simply call them inert gases, whereas in fact they are far from inert, they have their part to play, otherwise they would not be here doing their job of work. So, of course conditions in the Earth will change as the progression of mankind will change.

Always then there is change, for without change there is no progress. Mother Earth will be here until such time as she has fulfilled her reason for being, until she has evolved into such a state that then there would be no point in her being. You also would have evolved and you would be involved in other work in the cosmos,you see, with a different form and different conditions and you will take your higher knowledge to that part of the cosmos to help that progress.

SUSAN

I read in a recent article that someone said - is the green-house effect a real phenomenon and if it is what is the lesson in it for us? If it is why would someone else say it is not real, that it's a lie?

AT-HLAN

It is interesting at a different level to change our perceptions as to what is real and what is not real. You see, upon the planet Earth mankind can think about a theory or having a feeling and if enough people ponder and give that theory life then it becomes real, do you see? The green-house effect has been exacerbated somewhat by pollutants of carbon dioxide and so on. The Earth itself is undergoing changes and what mankind can do to alter the evolutionary chain of which the Gaia Tellus, the Earth, is part, is minimal. So in a sense there are man made solutions which do not help, but given the total overall evolutionary process of the Earth and the planets of this part of the Cosmos, it is like a drop in the ocean. If you think back to the times, in the towns for example, when humans burnt wood and coal, the fossil fuels, then there was more pollution in some ways than there is at the moment. There will be changes in the polarity of the Earth, there will be climactic changes. You will find again that the icecaps will change as it has done throughout the evolutionary process and progress of this tiny planet. So I would not wish for you to say that it does not matter, it has minimal effect on the overall plan.

You see, the great minds of guides and councillors from the Cosmos are working all the time upon the future progress, not just on the souls of these beings which you call humankind, but on the larger areas of which this tiny planet is a part and nothing will change that plan. All that will happen is that we will maximise that which you call spiritual beings to participate in the future rather than leaving them behind to start all over again. That is part of the Great Plan. The more advanced beings that can go forward in the evolutionary process, the greater and more effective is the evolutionary process. So you could say that if all the Spiritual evolution, the Cosmic evolution, the evolution of the souls of mankind would cease then it would take longer for other parts of the Plan to establish themselves and to grow. For there is much work to do on a cosmic level, do you see? The expansion of the Universe as you see it is not by chance, it is part of an overall plan and, in millions of years time,(we are heading for the future here lady Susan) we would like you to be around to be part of that process; for when this process reaches it's maximum expansion, then from that will be worked, at a different time and space, another Universe and so on, with different beings. So the thing gets more and more complex but never ceases to grow in one way or another. WOW!!

It would seem quite logical that we may choose to maximise our own potential abilities, to become a positive influence in the overall plan, to 'tune in' to the spiritual/cosmic network of communication using the vibration of unconditional love or be left behind to participate in subsequent cyclical evolutionary progression - perhaps!

TIM

I understand that a being comes to the earth and chooses it's own set of experiences, does Mother Earth also choose her own set of experiences and is there any such thing as an S.O.S. call in cosmic terms.

AT-HLAN

I can tell you that, first of all, we choose to incarnate upon the earth plane, we choose the conditions under which we incarnate. You must also realise that you incarnate, some of you, with great experience, some with not so much experience, it depends upon Cosmic influences and Earthly influences, and planetary influence also, which is why so many people are interested at this moment in their horoscopes. But you choose the circumstances that you find are appropriate for your progression. Added to this you also have freedom of choice, you are, at this time under these conditions, the only people in this galaxy who have this freedom of choice. So it is possible for you to both progress and regress, for some have taken on themselves difficult conditions, those in which they wish to teach the parents or the relatives of that particular soul. Sometimes these conditions become too oppressive so they choose the left hand pathway instead of the righthand pathway and so they have to come back to relearn that lesson.

The Great Spirit of the Mother Earth, Gaia, is an entity who is connected with the planetary system in which she finds herself and she can never be destroyed by mere earthly souls, this is an impossibility for you must remember, the influence of the higher mind and the great beings who always are aware, many of whom have been here for the earth as she is called, was founded in the first instance, and produced for you to progress at this level of experience.

So, there is an increase of awareness in mankind at the moment, for you must know that although there are thoughts that she is being destroyed, there are also great thoughts that she is being supported in many ways that would never have occurred to mankind if you had gone back, shall we say, one hundred years. You must also remember that this great Earth Mother is also evolving herself and she has undergone so many changes of fire, of flood, of ice, of cold. So, if you put all of these things into perspective then the changes brought about by mankind are as a drop in the ocean of the process of evolution.

HANNAH

Is mankind's higher consciousness and spirituality happening quickly enough in regard to the urgent needs of this planet. What can we do to turn the tide of the threat to this planet?

AT-HLAN

We are doing that which, under these conditions on our plane of existence, you people do under similar conditions in your personal and group meditations. This has a positive effect on the whole consciousness of the planet. You see, the positive and the negative thoughts and feelings of people form what has been termed as the psychosphere of the planet. Also, there is the consciousness of the planet itself, with the influence of the other planets and solar systems. So there are many, many, different impressions being made upon mankind from near and far.

The acceleration at the present time has been picked up from many more people than you would imagine. The problem we have at the moment is that other conditions impinge upon this acceleration for the individual, which is why you have an increased sensitivity both to the positive and to the negative and that is another reason why what you call 'guides' and influences are being brought in so that many people do see perhaps, not a guide, but what they term as a doorkeeper, in increasing numbers , for we are very concerned that we have as many positive influences around as possible. Those who seek the Light and evolution of the soul of mankind will act upon the individual and for a group soul, and, if you like, a national soul and for the soul of this planet. So sometimes it gets rather confusing, some people tune into this acceleration and do well, others use it for the wrong purpose.

There is a general acceleration, a learning period, so that people are more clearly coming to recognise what is beyond the spiritual level. They are beginning to accept that there are influences across the Cosmos. So what you are doing is helping that process, but it is also possible that some groups of souls will find the Light, will find themselves for example, able to travel to learn to influence other groups of souls who will follow a downward path, who will ignore these intelligences and will become grey areas.

Our home circle constantly receives information from At-hlan, spiritual guides and cosmic beings, referring to a cosmic force or energy that is inter-penetrating the earth's field and influencing those who are in tune with spiritual progression. Not only does this lead to accelerated learning (through various guides) but enables individuals to 'get through a lot of bad stuff' quite quickly, usually a painful process, so that they are in a position to participate fully in the eventful changes to come in the near future. In other words individuals may have had a difficult, even traumatic, life from a young age but, having overcome great difficulties in this incarnation they may have balanced their karma and so will be enabled to further progress and participate fully in the next part of the upward evolutionary cycle that seems to have begun.

HANNAH

Could you explain the term 'psychosphere' please?

AT-HLAN

Lady Hannah, it is not a bike upon which you ride I can assure you! You see, you have a body, you have an etheric body, you have a mental and emotional body, you have a cosmic or astral body and so on and so forth. When you pass into the next plane of existence you leave behind a material body and you take with you the etheric body. Many of you have also left behind the etheric and travel distances on a finer vibration, it is not, as is taught, a natural or logical progression. However.... I am interested in that so I divert from my own train of thoughts.

The planet, the material planet on which you live, also has these bodies. It has a mental, emotional body, which we sometimes call the psychosphere, for it contains its own reaction to whatever happens on or to it, whether it is beautifying, or edifying or if it is destructive or polluting. So the planet has its bodies and through your bodies you send out your notes, your colours, your tune, as does the Goddess Gaia. For the earth sends out its note, it's colour, its sound and so at this moment in time and over a longer period of time we come to help so that you can accelerate the learning process so that you cease to destroy that which is part of your own progression, part of your own soul evolution, it should be linked with you in harmony.

The Influence of Animals and Dolphins

SUSAN

I was wondering what purpose animals have in our lives.

AT-HLAN

First of all on a wider dimension, there are many forms upon the planet Gaia Tellus, which reflects the immensity of thought that has been given to the environment in terms of the multiplication of life forms, of beauty which is tangible for the higher life forms to appreciate. It is true at one stage in the evolutionary chain these animals did not fight or eat each other, but you will have to go back an awfully long way. So, linked with that there is the fact that there was a falling out between the animal kingdom and the next spiritual plane and above that which is the human kingdom, and so instead of having mental appreciation and a sympathetic relationship man killed animals. This was passed on in the aura and changed the animal chain and so it is the influence of mankind which has made animals develop in the sense that they kill each other for food. As a result of this there are still noble human beings who want to have a close relationship with the animal kingdom. You have what you would call household pets, and this becomes a mutual appreciation society and an almost symbiotic relationship where one helps the other. Has it not been said that when people get stressed and stroke their cat or dog then it relieves stress, so one helps the other do you see?

PATSY

Dolphins, there is always such interest and love for dolphins. Could you tell us their origins and their purpose for being here with us. We have read that they are re-incarnated Atlanteans, is this correct.?

AT-HLAN

Well, I would not like to disagree with anyone else's theory. There is much that is correct written in that particular book. I feel there was some sub-conscious interference and what happened to that channel was that they allowed the conscious to intercede somewhat. So you see, going back to the legend of Atlantis disappearing beneath the waves with all the stories of mermaids and fish people and so on, you have an almost natural transference of that into the theory that dolphins have Atlantean incarnations as their souls. This is not so, it is perpetuating a myth and a legend, if you understand my meaning. The dolphins do have great souls, great communicators, much love and they do come from a far distant planet, in Altair. They come to help with the evolution of the aquatic forms of life and they are enabled to have telepathic links with humans which has been documented when they have saved a drowning person. For example, they have sent signals to those who are mentally confused or backward, they have this capacity. The higher spirits of the dolphins will not remain upon the earth Plane for so much longer, although the animals, the beast, the entities, the flesh themselves, will continue here for their job on the Earth Plane; the reason why they were sent here is nearly complete. That is not a sadness, that is a rejoicing. It means to say that they have reached a time in their evolution when they may be released from that employment to work in another planetary system.

PATSY
So do they have a group soul or do they have individual souls like us?

AT-HLAN
You are part of a group soul of the planet of the Earth Plane. They are part of the group soul of dolphins, but they are also individuals, very much so. They have varying individuality, personal characteristics within that group soul. Their group soul is different from all the other aquatic marine life. They are a distinct group who have incarnated for that purpose from a far distant planet.

Whatever questions or series of questions are asked concerning whatever topic or aspect of life, then At-hlan, almost automatically, places the answers in a cosmic perspective, inasmuch as he refers to past, present and future. his teachings do not concern merely 'here and now' but how all relates to a positive and on-going plan. We may slow our own evolutionary cycle or even occasionally divert it (part of the learning process) but ultimately and of necessity it will proceed to its zenith under Divine Law.

PATSY

Regarding the animals changing, in past transcripts it has been said that the Whales are actually going to withdraw from this planet because mankind has not really acknowledged why it has come here as a gift, a special gift to us all.

AT-HLAN

They have been mis-used and abused. This was, as I remember correctly, the same as stated by 'White Feather'. In a sense White Feather was correct. There is much of your past lives stored in the Dolphin and the Whale. They have very long memories and usually a long life too, unless the life is curtailed by the sorrow and destruction of the worst kind performed by mankind. Over a period of time you will find that they will diminish. They will become rather scarce and a rarity. I do not myself see them disappearing completely for they are tuned into a network of re-creation and pro-creation which is necessary for the influences they have upon the Earth plane. It will be more that the higher souls of the species will depart. They will become removed in influence; it is very difficult to explain; they will still have a soul, a higher self, the being of those species will trans-migrate and take root in another part of the Universe with other beings. The lower soul will be left here until such time as those higher influences of the soul may rejoin them, but that is the choice of mankind.

PATSY

What sort of influences do Dolphins have, a lot of us have affinities with them, but we are not sure why?

AT-HLAN

They are empowered with vast networks of communication. They are the most communicative beings on the Earth plane. In terms of distance they can send a thought a thousand miles and it will be picked up immediately. They have a family life based upon much love. This love may also extend a thousand miles or more. They can hear and appreciate each other at such a distance, where as human beings who have had such a communication network have lost theirs to a large extent. We are, with help from such people as you and those who wish to come and help under the protection of the White Brotherhood, re-establishing that possibility, that fact. As you know, you have communicated with beings from hundreds of light years away, this is a part of your brain, your mind and your soul which is there, which contains these possibilities. So in perspective, although it may seem astounding for a whale or a dolphin to communicate at such a distance, you can better this yourselves!

I found it quite difficult to accept the first channeling concerning dolphins, particularly as I didn't have a belief in their supposed special attributes and therefore, some months later, when other similar questions arose, I battled subconsciously against the replies that At-hlan wished to communicate; as they say, - the truth will out!

The Extinction of the Dinosaurs

LENETTE
Why did the dinosaurs die off?

AT-HLAN
The dinosaurs had reached their limits of progression and the Earth Mother and the influences around the Earth changed. There was a step forward in the process of evolution, even now there are animal kingdoms that die out, not necessarily because of the influences of man, but because they have used up their useful purpose. Tying in with this, what accelerated the changes was indeed a large comet, no wrong, a meteorite, a very large meteorite which was half a mile across. And so at the same time this accelerated the changes in the atmosphere and the temperature of the Earth Plane. You see, what would have been the point in these animals proceeding when they had ecologically and symbiotically helped with the process of the evolution of the planet. And so, although you have remnants from millions of years ago left, with Iguana and so forth, they primarily had become stultified and stopped. They were not in a position to adapt to the changing climate, to the changing vibration and so their souls left the Earth Plane in a comparatively short space of time, to re-emerge in different life forms, in, if you like, more modern life forms, not necessarily on this planetary surface but upon others and to be put into those life forms where progress could have been made.

You see, when you have such a great meat eater as the Tyrannosaurus Rex, or the herbivorous Iguanadon, they had reached the end of their progression, there was no where for them to go under those conditions. And so, they say, it is a combination of influences. They had reached the end of their progression and could not evolve further on the Earth Plane so circumstances were brought to bear which permitted them to leave, to die out, and this was a release you see. It was not something to be remorseful about, so they were released to progress under different circumstances. And so the climatic conditions, for a time, changed upon the Earth Plane and mankind progressed in this soul evolution. I think that has answered your question so far Lady Lenette.

116

LENETTE
Yes, thank you At-Hlan.

HANNAH
Hello At-Hlan

AT-HLAN
Good afternoon Lady Hannah, it is nice to see that your life is progressing.

HANNAH
Yes, I feel so, thank you. To follow with that question, were there humans with the dinosaurs?

AT-HLAN
Oh, indeed there were humans with dinosaurs. They were contemporaneous for a time. In fact they were one time in Atlantis, where the Dinosaurs were domesticated and used to carry cargoes and so forth. But they were in a sense not compatible. It would have been no good for mankind to have used these animals in this way, for again it would have slowed the progress of mankind and the Dinosaurs had come to the end of their use. But you will find in your recorded history where there are both human beings and Dinosaurs living at the same time in the Atlantean period, which goes back of course many millions of years. Even your scientists will agree there were dinosaurs living 3 million years B.C. for example. It will be interesting that they will eventually find out that the species of mankind were far more diverse at that time than simple Cro-magnon or Neanderthal man who were different tribes living at the same time as the more cultured and sophisticated Atlanteans. But this will be discovered in the near future.

The scientific logic of the progressional evolution of mankind has never ceased to amaze me by its incredibly simple theories that, more recently, seem to be changing. Imagine if a being from Arcturus took an African pygmy captive as a prime example of 'man', and another person from Capella took hostage a nuclear physicist, and they then compared notes. What confusion! In a similar juxtaposition, At-hlan is alluding to the facts (as he sees them) that there were many 'facets' of human-kind who co-existed, having little in common at that time. The highly-civilised (for the most part) technologically advanced Atlanteans would have viewed cro-magnon man etc as primitive in the extreme. Putting things in perspective; long before 3,000BC the Egyptians flourished as a highly cultured people (a former Atlantean colony) while contemporaraneously other peoples still inhabited caves and other simple shelters.

KERRY

Going back to the humans and animals, in an ideal world we would like the different species to live in harmony, is this too much to expect or will it come at a later date?

AT-HLAN

No, it will come at some later stage. It has happened before hand that mankind and animals have lived in a state of peace and of mutual sharing and of symbiosis almost. That one can help the other to appreciate different things, the different senses, different ways of communication. This will re-occur at some stage in the development of mankind. We will find that animals will no longer destroy each other. There will no longer be the signals sent by mankind, the higher thought processes will no longer signal that this is the way. Mutual self destruction will cease after such a time when again such a lesson will be learned from mankind. They will look for a way forward and will be guided because they have asked. In the asking comes the giving and when the giving is accepted, then they live in harmony like your pet animals. Such animals absorb your influences, a signal sent out from you will bind animals closely to your aura when it is of love and caring. There is always a mutual respect and understanding between yourselves and the lower life forms. This will re-occur.

Cloning and Scientific progression

LENETTE
With all the genetic work that the scientists are doing what will be the outcome of things like 'clones'?

AT-HLAN
There have been many scientific discoveries which of course have all been known before hand. You have reached a point in your evolution where scientists have made such discoveries as of course were made in Atlantis and used adversely. Mixtures of human and animal forms were made, bestial forms that for a time became uncontrolled. This will not happen with your scientists today, for as you know, on this vibration there is great scientific knowledge going towards finding out how the Universe operates. For example, finding out how such things as quarks, background noise and black holes work and so on. The instrumentation is becoming sensitive enough for the scientists in the short term, in the not too distant future, to realise that life exists on so many different levels. It will take them eons to find out the complex network of existence.

They will in fact be tuned into their own spirituality and therefore processes such as cloning and genetic experimentation will be controlled by they themselves from their own personal insight, their own increasing psychic awareness. It will not be uncontrolled and will work at the level that will be best for mankind. The otherside of the coin is that in experimentation they will realise their own limitations and realise that they may misuse power or they may use it to shine the Light, even though that would not be their term of reference. There will be little to worry about, there will be a self control experimentation which will bring amazement to them as to the complexity and depth to their own existence. They will not wish to disrupt the flow of human life in the future of mankind.

HANNAH
Have clones got souls?

AT-HLAN

This would be a problem would it not. Under natural circumstances a soul comes into being in the natural course of events as soon as the sperm permeate the egg. It is an instantaneous birth, that is when the soul is incarnated at that time. Many people have written that the soul comes in at different times, that is the cojoining of the different genes and the genes are united when the soul enters, otherwise there would not be progression towards life as you know it. With cloning, by working at dividing, separating and putting together of genes only there would be a soul that comes in where there is potential for normal human life. Otherwise the combinations of chemicals and so on would die away. So it is possible for a soul to incarnate and to experience that different form. As I have said, when this happens the scientists having learned from that will not wish to proceed with a chemical approach to life, to lead to a 'cul de sac'. They will see that things may happen to them themselves that will open their eyes further. They will cease of their own permission to proceed in this direction.

The Evolution of Mankind and Environmental Changes

KERRY

I have heard that a change is occurring upon the Earth. Is it going to happen in three phases, the first beginning now and ending at the end of springtime. It is a kind of reconstruction of Mother Earth to enable us to become better informed. Do you know anything about this and if so what are your thoughts about it?

ÀT-HLAN

It is easy to talk about phases as people have done since history began, which is why they look at magical numbers and the rotation of the Earth in conjunction with various planets. The phase that we are undergoing at the moment in what you call the beginning of the Aquarian Age, has been going on for a number of years. It involves the influences of Cosmic beings. This phase in an ongoing phase, not for a few weeks or months but for hundreds, if not thousands of years. What your informers, your communicators are referring to is a fraction of that, a fraction of re-alignment of forces. For you see, there are ancient forces that are coming into being which used to be called magnetic lines, ley lines and so on. These are becoming more in tune with other planets and part of this system is the outside influences from other parts of this Universe, many of whom have been in this area in the formation of this solar system, as you call it. In the short term you will find that there will be many changes in mankind and there will be lines drawn, even though we do not wish this to happen, but they will be drawn so that those who wish Peace, Harmony and Joy may develop without the interference of those beings who do not wish this. This will take from three to five years, but the bigger changes will come to you in the era I have already described.

I am sorry to bore you with a repetition, so that the third phase will come after that and will last hundreds of years into the New Era where there will be life where people will be able to communicate telepathically. It is difficult for those entities who are on different levels above the evolution of the souls cycle of those upon the Earth plane, to be able to clearly translate in terms of time and space. As has been said before this is a manmade utensil to help cope with the Earthly existence that originally evolved around the seasons of the movement of the Sun and Moon. This is a phase that they are going through which will also change for it will no longer be necessary in the future.

There will be intuitive knowledge, there will be lightening of the heaviness, the feeling that the body is so compacted, so there will be bodies produced that find it easier to travel, lighter in terms of the heaviness in relation to the Earth plane, for the gravitational forces upon the Earth will be made lighter. Your scientists will be amazed at the changes in the pull of the Earth's gravity and so your bodies will be lighter and you will be able to travel further upon the Earth. You will also be able to travel away from your etheric bodies, that is the nearest I can describe that, your human bodies will be nearer the constitution of your etheric bodies, so you will be less prone to disease, for example, and you will be able to use telepathic communication, communication of the mind, and so the communication will be more clearly heard from the different levels of communication. I would not be able to say precisely more than I have said when these changes come about.

KERRY
We would like to know when will the human form change, for what reason and under what influence?

AT-HLAN
The human form will not change for eons in fact.What will happen is that the conditions around the human form, the environment will change. I have predicted for some time twenty or thirty years in the future that the conditions will change. They will change because of the frustration felt not only upon our planes of existence but upon the Earth plane. Materialism is not the way forward as it has seemed to become more self destructive and halts the progress of the creative side of the human mind. The creative side has progressed with many people, for there are more centres for alternative therapies, for meditations and so on than ever before in the western world. So the conditions will be so that the creative mind will be more easily accessible to both spiritual and cosmic influences which is the work we are undertaking at the moment.

The human form will exist much as it is for eons. It will eventually become lighter. It will not be so heavy or so dense, the bone structure will lighten. It will not be necessary as conditions upon the earth plane change, for that density of body to exist as it is at the moment. You will also find that because conditions have changed that again eons in the future, hundreds if not thousands of years, that the gravitational force upon the earth plane will become less. It will move towards half or less to what it is at the moment. There will be progression as many on the earth plane begin to see that the progression of mankind is tied to and inextricably bound up with the progression of the universe.

There will be an interrelationship between the beings 'in the flesh' as it were upon the earth plane the spirit plane and the cosmic plane also. This will take time. In the future the existence will be lighter airier and it will be easier for those who wish to communicate, to communicate. There will also be this unconscious longing to be fulfilled, it will be more and more conscious as Mankind begins to realise how it has been cut off from these modes of communication which existed in part of the Atlantian Empire. You are beginning to discover about the ancient Egyptians and to some extent the Babylonians. It goes back, properly interpreted, in the Hindu scriptures who knew of cosmic beings when God was not a figurehead, but beings from God from different parts of the Universe were messengers of Truth and Honesty.

The last two 'different' questions were put to At-hlan over one year apart and the answers are remarkably similar, supporting the truth enshrined in his teachings and also making the point clearly and, from his point of view, indisputably. It is questionable as to whether all people will follow this pathway, for it would appear that many, who absolutely refuse to use choice positively over many incarnations, may be afforded a less uplifting future experience.

KERRY
As a follow up does this mean that by the time the human form changes the vast majority of people that are on the earth plane will be more spiritually aware?

AT-HLAN
Yes, to put it simply. One cannot happen without the other. They will find that there are more positive and tangible evidences available to them. Many people will see this as a new beginning in the times that I have stipulated, I will say 2012-2016AD for the umpteenth time. That will just be the beginning of a change in the mode of thinking about who is Mankind, the reasons for existence and then perhaps they will begin to see the importance of their existence as well.

Therefore, see that the differences between the politics, the colour, the creed and the religions are totally insignificant and meaningless in comparison with the meaning of existence itself.

HANNAH

Does this mean that the youth will have clearer direction? We would hope that they will look to their parents or elders for guidance many seem so lost.

AT-HLAN

You must ask yourselves why some are not lost. My channel Rohann was reading to the Lady Kerry-Anne 'your children are not *your* children, they are the sons and daughters of God'. They are very open at this stage of your evolutionary cycle to suggestion and influence. They are much more open than they have been for thousands of years. Where there is a negative influence they will absorb almost fully that negative influence and commit acts which go against truth, righteousness and honesty. On the other hand there are many many more children who have been incarnating. They have been incarnating with parents who are trustworthy and trustful, who have some knowledge of the pathway. Even though they are not fully informed these parents are open themselves to suggestion and passing on good teachings to their children. They begin to realise that their children have more knowledge and truth in them than they do themselves. So we are at a time of many strides forward in a very short period of time in comparison to the last few thousand years. You can see how much knowledge has accumulated in the last two hundred years. This has been put rather more to the material rather than to spiritual use.

HANNAH

So we have great responsibilities.

AT-HLAN

Yes, indeed they are great responsibilities because for the first time we have seen very enlightened children. We have also experienced to our sorrow those children who at a very young age involved themselves in experiences of destruction. You must always remember that there are real negative influences as well as positive influences. This works at a cosmic level as well as an earthly or material level. So always there is a battle between the pathway of righteousness and that which leads down towards the depths of despair.

PATSY

When the changes occur in the human form, will changes also occur in the flora and fauna?

AT-HLAN

It is already changing in the flora and fauna of this planet due to the influence of mankind. You will find where there is a loss, there is replenishment, where there is death there is life, where there is despair there is hope. Sounds like a lecture by one of your priests does it not?! You must remember that at one time I was a priest myself. So, because of the changes upon the Mother Earth, Gaia Tellus herself, in the atmosphere around and in the changing of relationships with the planetary and the Cosmic influences, there will be indeed changes in some forms of life upon the Earth plane.Where species, to some extent disappear, new forms will be found. Mankind encourages new forms himself; if you look at the varieties of flowers and hybrids and so on. This is positive, but there will constraints upon the experimentation with human life. They will find to their own shock and horror that where they have broken Divine Law that there will be rather an unfortunate consequence that will stop them in experimentation which may lead to the bringing forth of a mutant, a strain of human being which has happened in the past, in the latter days of Atlantis. The time scale we are looking at here is, shall we say fifty or sixty years hence. The experimentation with the human could be earlier than that, the time when mankind will realise the error of his ways, with experimentation of human life and with animal life will come earlier than that. There will be new forms in the middle of the next century.

HANNAH

In other parts of the Universe do they use this human method to reproduce?

AT-HLAN

Never, no, in different parts of the Universe there are different processes of production and reproduction of certain species. Sometimes the environment plays a large part, sometimes the mental, emotional field plays a large part, Always it is done with love and the transference of love, not just with the people concerned but through the people concerned. Of course you are channels at the point of allowing the possibility of a new soul to incarnate. Love is channelled through you . When the soul arrives already there is a network, a programme, an environment into which this soul is projected, otherwise it could not exist.

The diversity of question and answer in this chapter - from dinosaurs to cloning - tends to leave me breathless even on re-reading! The information received manages to completely cut across preconceived ideas, destroying stereotype and replacing it with a multitude of possibilties while simultaneously managing to form a cohesive philosophy. It is remarkable how the information goes far beyond any of my own 'reasoned' thoughts and ideas and, indeed, throws conventional, even unconventional, thinking into a fair amount of confusion. But the questions are answered firmly and without evasion, bringing in a holistic approach that, quite logically, links us to everything in the universe because we are cosmic beings that have a relationship with everything, at whatever level of experience. The more we open our minds and allow ourselves to become part of the flow of life, the further we will develop and become attuned to Universal consciousness.

LENETTE

I have been reading a lot about the end of this century and going into the age of Aquarius, it is very worrying because people like Nostradamus and Ramala say we are going to change an awful lot. Do you have any ideas on that?

AT-HLAN

Yes indeed. There is some Truth based on the ages of Pisces and Aquarius and so on, for the Earth has natural cycles as has the Moon, Sun, Stars etc. and we have already thought ourselves ahead of the question and would give you the times of 2012-2016AD, when there will be changes and a breakdown in the monetary system - things will change very quickly there - when philosophies will change very quickly, there will be individual struggles and group struggles, where there will be changes in the Earth's atmosphere. It is all very worrying, is it not? It has happened time and time again, for you know that the polarity of the Earth has been reversed three times. There used to be 360 days to the year but the rate of vibration of the Earth has been increased to 365 days in the year. There have been glacials and inter-glacials, there have been times when there has been little or no ozone and times when it has been very heavy. Sometimes these things happen naturally, sometimes as a result of what is happening on

Gaia herself. Every action has a re-action, is a basic scientific truth is it not so? So you have many changes to look forward to in your lives, indeed you are part of those changes at the present time. So, many more people are asking questions about cosmic entities, have seen things, phenomena. How many people do you know who are interested in spiritual phenomena and matters of the Astral in comparison with 10 years ago, have they not multiplied ten fold?

The Future of the Earth and its Place in the Universe

GLORIA

There is a new school of Thought and Light. This school tries to give light to the Earth, it is said that in about 4 years time the Earth is going to go through a metamorphosis from a third to a fifth dimension. There will be an ascension of enlightened beings who will ascend and return as Masters to be of assistance. Is there any truth in this?

AT-HLAN

Throughout the history of this planet there have been sects and religions who have prophesied such things in one way or another. Sometimes there is Truth in these prophesies and it is not my responsibility or my approach or way to disagree what others prophesy. My own Truth, that has been said before is that the year 2000 will pass peacefully and tranquilly. In the year 2012 to 2016 there will be changes upon the Earth plane which will not encompass fire and brimstone, will not bring about chaos and despair for most, for there is no point. It will bring about changes in awareness, heightened awareness. Those who have been involved in gross materialism in using money as their God will find that they have lost their way and will find the pointlessness of it all. Indeed, the monetary system will be changed, the process of this has been going on for sometime now. The planetary changes in Jupiter are part of that network that will alter the perceptions of mankind, but the climax will not be until that time that I have told you. I will not as a general rule give forecasts or prophesy for there is no point because you see even at this level there maybe brought about changes that do not bring about the prophesied time, place or procedures. Of these times I have said I have been very firm about. You will find that we do not go from the third to the fifth dimension because this would interfere with Universal Law*. The vibration of the Earth, rather like Jupiter, will be changed somewhat. You will find that somehow you feel lighter, that things of the spirit and the cosmic energies become more real, more tangible more touchable.

So, I sympathise with this sect but would not entirely agree, although they do seem to have some influence that is truthful. Information that is received can only be relayed depending upon the channel and perhaps sometimes by sub-conscious interference by the mind of the person themselves. There are as you know many people who are channeling entities both of a spiritual and cosmic nature upon the Earth plane at the moment. There are films made to do with the after-life, to do with ghosts and extra-terrestrials. This is not by chance, it is that these creative people are using the right hand way to pick up the messages that are more prevalent now than at any time over the last 5000 years. You have gone through a period where things of a spiritual nature should have been very important but of course the truths therein have been perverted by various religions and sects. Perhaps from the very highest point of view based on creedalism. We come here with Truths that are not based on any doctrines or 'isms' or even 'ologies'!

We have come to realise that if time/space is the fourth dimension, then telepathic thought and travel (like astral travel) are about the fifth dimension of awareness. We will not be fifth dimensional people in the flesh, but more people will use the fifth dimensional capacity with which we, or many of us, are endowed at the present time. There will be more mass communication using mind-thoughts and an increasing awareness of making links with extra-terrestrial beings.

JAQUELINE

What is this overall feeling that I get, and I am sure that others do to, when they see something that is very beautiful in nature for example a landscape, something out of the sea. It is the most overwhelming feeling of joy, a soul experience.

AT-HLAN

Indeed it is to do with soul awareness, Mother Earth is a very important planet even though it is on an arm of a spiral of a galaxy. It was placed there for the reasons that it would be interfered with less and there was more opportunity of protecting it's environment, for you see, although we shine the light always there are adverse forces.

Upon this planet you have a larger variety of plant life, of insect life, of animal life, a wider range of colours, more varied vibrations that these give out than on any single planet in the whole of the Universe that you perceive. There are other Universes working at different vibrations that your scientists have not yet perceived. In the United States of America they are beginning to realise this, for they are using especially adapted telescopes with listening and sighting information. These instruments are beginning to pick up sights and sounds of what are considered to be invisible objects.

You are placed here for a great reason, you have the potential of great powers when they are used for the right reason to influence other planetary systems and other galaxies. This is because you have a brain which is capable of doing this, although your scientists do not know the why and the wherefore of seventy-five per-cent of the use of your brain. It is tied up with the giving, receiving and sending of information, not just upon this planet but to be linked with other planetary systems in other galaxies. This is part of your potential, your soul evolution. There are times in your lives when there is a deep inner recognition of the wonder that is placed before you and a deep recognition that you are indeed privileged to be here at moments in time to perceive it at different levels in all it's wonder, it's poetry and beauty.

PATSY

So where will the spirit of Gaia Tellus go then if she comes to the end of her evolution?

AT-HLAN

Well, this will be carried with all the influences, knowledge and experience in all probability, with a new star influence. It will be taken and used in a new planetary system. It may interest you to know that sometimes stars are brought into an area and then planets are brought to that star, so it is not always the same sort of system. Some of your planets have come from the core of your solar sun; in other systems, but not in all of them, you have a star brought to influence who has got the correct influence and the spirit of Mother Earth would be linked to that star system and would help to form the planets. Sometimes the planets would be taken from the material from the star, but sometimes they are brought from other stars and put in place, because that is the best way to balance that system.

PATSY

I have read in books that eventually Masters and Angels will walk the Earth with us. Is this true?

AT-HLAN

Well, there are Masters and Angels walking with you in this time and this place, you see. For those with 'the eyes to see and the ears to hear'; - what is meant by that is that with the progression and changes in the physical or apparent physical evolution of mankind it will be easier to perceive, to see more tangibly and to hear more coherently as well. In the evolutionary stages of course it will be easier to see what you call Angels who are beings from another planet, and cosmic Masters and Cosmic beings who are influences in your circle. You have reached the stage of evolution where you can see, hear or be impressed or be aware of their presence. As mankind progresses more and more human people in the fleshly body will be able to sense and see these beings which are here and now. Under these circumstances it is not such a shock to the system because it is already happening, already happened, it is just a state of mankind, when it is too dense, when it is too material, then you have retrograde steps, when the bestial rather than the spiritual manifests itself. We are reaching the Aquarian age, place or stage, when this can be felt more easily and seen more frequently. For the many, always there are those who will not progress or refuse the guidance, fail to see the light. It is their choice.

JILL
Does the Universe go on forever, or does it end somewhere?

AT-HLAN
Which Universe, the ones that you have seen or the ones you do not see? You see there is Alpha and Omega, there is the Great Mind, the Central Intelligence and while you progress and you feed back love so is the Universe, and the Universe is always in a state of progression, always in a state of balancing the disharmony and the harmony and so there is perpetual growth. There exists time and space without time and space, there is only space where material exists to give it the name 'space', where there is nothing there is still something, that something is invisible, cannot be seen, but it is not a space, it is a place before existence that is waiting to come into being.

There is no ending for there is no beginning, there is not, as Einstein said, a start, so that you would progress as you think in a straight line and return to the place at which you started. This is not true and will be disproven by the scientists at some time in the future. But you see, in the same way you are a soul who has potential, you may not feel the potential but there are buds waiting to flower, they may not yet exist as buds but they are there in your future if you wish them to be there. So, if you make your choice, if you choose the pathway of enlightenment so a bud comes into being and that bud grows and sounds it's note and it affects the growth and spirituality of Ancient Wisdom of others, so it is with the Universe.

The Future

PATSY

Roger asked us to ask you about the future. We couldn't actually think of a specific question so we wondered if you would let us know about it please!!? (loads of laughter - particularly from At-Hlan!)

AT-HLAN

That is the most non-specific question that has ever been asked! But when you listen back to your recording you will find that I have already been answering that question about the future of mankind. So, in a sense, I have beaten you to it! I have already been discussing the future of mankind and the part that you and millions of others will play in the evolution of mankind. You see it has been said before in these recordings that your soul did not start millions of years ago, - 15 million years ago or so - upon the Earth Plane, it was sent to you. The Great Mind who is at the centre of all creation, and of whom we are all part at our varying levels of complexity, has sent your souls to you, directly or indirectly, through the Ministry of Angels, through your inspirers, with your guides and inspirers and such people as the White Brotherhood, who were here before the physical concept of the world was here. In the beginning indeed was God , but also through God, The Great Mind, The Great White Father, who was sending beings to oversee the planetary system and it's formation and it's relationship with the Galaxy and the stars and so on.

And so you came from a distance, you were already part of the Universe when you arrived here, although after a time, through establishing the bodily form from the Cosmic form, although it is called the spiritual form, it was indeed a Cosmic form, the early Cosmic pioneers adapted a fleshy overcoat and that did not work out too well in the beginning. So further cosmic influences were sent to help with the process. I must say that it has been said that there is some sort of Galactic Game going on here which is ridiculous when we look through the eyes of Cosmic influences and we see that souls are sent here to combine with other influences, other souls to help those impoverished souls to experience the fullness of evolution upon the Earth Plane with it's diversity of emotion. It is only here where there is such diversity of emotion, of plant life, animal life and so on. And so it is a great area for soul growth, for experiencing the possibility of a full potential. So here there may be many Cosmic Masters, and higher beings in the making,and have been in the making and have already been sent out from this planet.

I think that has answered your question, but...(At-Hlan pauses)...this is very important. I am being given other information along these lines.. Which is to try and release from mankind the whole idea that they were born here and will live and die here. They were not born here, they came from the Great Mind and there are twelve Extra-Terrestrial or Star influences upon this planet and with the Solar Logos, the Star, the God of this planetary system this makes 13 influences. And as we progress upon this vibration in which you have felt mainly the influence of that Star which you call the Sun, now you are beginning to feel also in your progression the influence of Sirius and Polaris, and of Altair, Aldebaran, Betlegeuse and Castor and Pollux and so on. I am being given all these Star systems you see, and as you progress so the influence of the Stars will be felt more strongly as they send out their information and they contact you on a higher conscious level, which has so far been only on a sub-conscious level, and as your vibration is raised so you will feel it on a super-conscious level.

Which is why, Lady Patsy, we have refered to you as a Star Child, for you feel these influences very strongly and it is all part of the system that you express. And so, at that level you envisage and visualise the guides that you draw for others, do you see, so you are tuned in to this mighty network which comes closer when you allow it to. But also you are empowered so to do through work that you do and the beliefs that you have and the commitment to the Truth... my channel seems to be conducting an orchestra!... but it is very important and uplifting is it not.

As well as having a remarkable sense of humour, particularly when conversing with those he knows well, At-hlan has, as we have come to accept, a memory of just about every word that has been communicated through his channel, Rohann, and he constantly seeks ways and means of explaining that 'human beings' are an important part of a system and integral to it. We are beginning to find out that we are not part of a Galactic game but that we have the responsibility for realising our own positive potential, certainly in shaping the future of mankind at different levels of experience and, indirectly therefore, we may have the ability to influence the evolution of the Universe.

Chapter 7   *The Influences of Egypt and Atlantis*

Contents

Why Pyramids as Cosmic Centres of Communication?

PATSY

The pyramids in Egypt is another area that fascinates not just us but a lot of other people generally. Can we have some more information on them as to their use. In particular does each pyramid have the same use or are they used for different ceremonies.?

AT-HLAN

This is a most interesting question because people were impressed to build pyramids as a focus for power, for a focus for intelligence, for meeting places in the early days. There were different influences with these different meeting places. Of course it is possible to communicate under certain conditions without these inter-galactic focal points, but you will find certain types of buildings from different types of materials on other planets as well. They were focused not just to receive information and power but to transmit it as well. In Atlantis there was a two way communication between the various inter-galactic extra-terrestrial people and those who were given such powers upon the Earth Plane. It is of great interest to you, for the pyramids that were built at Giza were built there both to receive and to send out signals. The substance of the White Marble overlaid the pyramids and gold was used at it's peak, for these to send out a beacon not just in the daytime but at night time also. The materials used there had a power, as it were, all of their own. Messages could be sent to the priesthood and the initiates who could send information to certain star systems in the universe. There was much progression in the early days of Egypt, but those times will come again, for you see there was an erosion of powers that were given at a high level.

Again mankind decided to use them for the wrong reasons and to build such pyramids to their own glory rather than the original purpose. These proliferated to smaller kingdoms. There were disruptions and fighting between different factions of these peoples so that eventually the power was taken away completely and they became imitations and empty shells. The knowledge that was disseminated there has been given to you and Rohann and others who sit in your circle, which is why you can go back with many people who come here and other places and know that they have had an Egyptian incarnation. Knowledge and wisdom is never lost, but sometimes passed on from an area that is full of war to an area that is full of peace so that the people there may use this power for the highest Truths, which seems to me to be quite sensible does it not?

PATSY

So over a period of time that sort of power would be re-established?

AT-HLAN

That sort of power is already being re-established, but it will not be necessary to build buildings, for again we have to learn as well, as you have had to learn, that the greatest establishment of higher thoughts and communications systems at it's highest level, is through people rather than places. Cathedrals and Temples have been built, but this has not been the way forward for a long time. Again you have created a hierarchy of priests who have no power because they do not work for the dissemination of all knowledge, for all of mankind, but merely a sect, which is not good. They then find the alters they have built are desecrations of the name of the Almighty, The Great Mind, and Primal Order. So it will be the future of the places and people who come together who sit and who share the information, to share love and bring upliftment. Sometimes this was done, as it were, behind closed doors, but we see that in the near future it will not need be so.

PATSY

So in effect we are the pyramids and temples of today.

AT-HLAN

Indeed, you are absolutely correct. You have a great responsibility. On the other hand those people who take this responsibility have in a way been chosen, have been given the stages of development to use for the correct purposes. Still the system may be flawed for they can always turn, of their own choice, to the left hand path, for the downward path instead of the right hand or the upwards path.

It is worth noting here that energy is being withdrawn from orthodox religions because of the misuse of power, that is still turning potential love to hate and envy, and the Master Initiates are now beginning to empower groups and individuals within groups, who sit for the highest reasons, to become part of the communication network of Universal Truth and to link with others, from the spiritual and cosmic realms to assist in the upward spiral of knowledge and understanding. In this way we help the progression and evolution of mankind and we begin to 'find' ourselves not only at a spiritual level of experience but as 'star seeds', as part of the influence in the universe.

PATSY

How come the pyramids are so massive?

AT-HLAN

It is a question of the stages of development of mankind at that particular time. You must remember that these were also used in Atlantis. You still find them in Mayan and Aztec times and so on. They go back far further than the scientists have shown, to 20,000 - 30,000 B.C. You can only work on the knowledge of the past and how things were constructed. They were re-established in Egypt because this was the means of communication which had been brought about in Atlantis and of a continuation of that. There were high hopes that even the destruction of one cultural system that another cultural system would be re-established. It would rise to the point of wisdom of that culture and eventually temples would become temples of love, temples of sacrifice of worldly thoughts. It would not be sacrifice of people; of course they became places where people were buried and initiates were killed in many cases through lack of true power, through mis-use of power.

If you go back to the times before the building of the temples the power was given and the earthly bodies constructed to deal with the conditions of the planetary system and of the gravities and magnetic fields of the Earth. There was a time when the temples were not used for worship but they were used as a focus for the mental abilities in the physical, for this was deemed to be necessary at that particular time. It is quite difficult to explain but my helpers have said that because the soul was developed in a physical body and that the challenges were laid out both physical and mental, to develop the soul further to bring love, then there was a time when the body and the soul needed to find a focus in the early development and some of these temples were built.

Although you have mis-used some of the material gifts, there have been people over millions of years who have sat for the development of the soul, of pure thought and universal consciousness. This has now been disseminated to enough peoples at such a level that it is not a necessity to build these material places as a focus to contact all the influences, or at least many of the influences that have been or will be upon the planet Earth. So you can sit in your circles and undoubtedly contact these influences. You have not needed to have built a shrine, temple or a pyramid but merely to have sat for Truth.

PATSY

You mentioned Khufu and Menes. As you know, I have drawn a picture of Khufu. There is really nothing I can find to read about him.. could you give us some information please.

AT-HLAN

My channel was talking about being 'low profile' about an hour ago, was he not, Khufu is a shortened name of that entity who was surrounded, as you would say, in the magical mists of time. Who was an Avatar, who protected himself from adverse influences and worked quietly here and there. Infact, he could project himself over great distances whilst being in one place. He could simultaneously transfer himself to many places, as in fact you do when you are linked into the network of thought transference. You may take part of your energy and be an influence a great distance away from your body, as all of you should understand. It is part of your work that you do when you send out thoughts. At that level you become part of someone elses life and an influence perhaps hundreds or thousands of miles away. There would not have been much written or graphically detailed about this entity . Having known the misuse of power, again, this was a higher evolved soul who came to bring peace and harmony.

He was a soul who helped link the two tribes of Egypt, the Upper and Lower parts of Egypt. He could be in Heliopolos and Alexandria simultaneously, and at Memphis and so on. The work that went on was one of great forces of the Earth Mother, the Spiritual and Cosmic forces.Much work was done in building a special monument and much of that was secret and hidden from the eyes of mankind so that it could not be misused. That power still is there, in Egypt, and we see the Light shining from that special place where the magnetic lines of the Earth cross most strongly.Not always do you need the presence of man in the physical but this is visited by those from the spiritual and cosmic worlds. Although I say 'spirit and cosmic', of course at a certain level one becomes the other as it were and both combine to do both kinds of work, spiritual work for the Earth Mother that links automatically with the cosmic experiences of these people. I have had to rely on my other informants more strongly in answer to that question because some information is given to me that either is beyond my recall or has been outside of my terms of reference. Now I also have that knowledge, so you see we all learn together sometimes.

142

HANNAH
The Staff of Life, I have read about it's Divine and Cosmic influences, will it always be in the safe keeping of the Masters?

AT-HLAN
Well you see there is no such thing as a single Staff of Life. There are the powers that emanate through beings who have Staffs for different reasons and purposes. These Staffs become a focus of many influences, they will pick up cosmic and earthly influences and those of the White Brotherhood know of these Staffs of Light which have been used by the Masters. They may look as if they are made of wood or ebony or metal or whatever to, as it were, the human eye. They have been used for millennia, for the powers of good, for the powers of disseminating knowledge. They are fountains of love and in your meditations often you will see fountains, fountains of love. These Staffs may work on different levels of being with that person. Unfortunately there are always Staffs that have negative influences, and so you may have seen described in your films such as 'Darth Vadar'and so on where the battles between good and bad are seen. Then sometimes these Staffs bring in positive and negative influences and they form a focus where these battles sometimes take place,these are only under certain conditions. Great have been these battles.

There are some of these Staffs that are unseen by the Human eye, yet seen on a higher level of being that you have all seen. Sometimes they lose their power, sometimes they transform or transpose their power into something else. You see, also crystals have been used for similar purposes, for they are able to store great power. So, there is no one Staff of Life or Light, but there are many used for different purposes at different times. It would be impossible to confer upon one person, one being, whatever level of awareness that they were at, all the Life Forces, all the energies, all the potential progress into the future because however much protection may be given and surrounding that person it still may not be part of the overall Universal Plan. Great power may corrupt the person or may have a corruptive influence upon those who surround that person, to make them envious or jealous and to misuse that power.

PATSY
To carry on with our Egyptian questions from last week.. Why are the pyramids in the configuration of Orions belt?

AT-HLAN

The influences of what is called 'the belt of Orion' goes back earlier to the Atlantean civilisation and the three major stars in that system were relevant to what the Atlanteans would consider to be, what you would call 'the Father, the Son and the Holy Ghost'. Of course this changed with the mythology of the Egyptians, but that was transposed over from Atlantis to the colony of Egypt and then was added other configurations. So, simply that was it. Also of course there were very strong influences in the Atlantean civilisation from those star systems, so there was a relationship between the Atlanteans and those star systems, as strong as you might consider your relationship to the Siriuns. Part of the mythology of the Atlanteans and the Egyptians was based on what they considered to be beings from those worlds, those systems, if you like. So that was the centre of, or starting point from which all other configurations arose.

PATSY

The first star in the 'Belt', Alnitak, that is the one that actually links with one of the shafts in the Kings Chamber, the other one is Sirius. Is there a particular reason for that?

AT-HLAN

If you consider there were relationships between Alpha Draconis, Polaris and so on, of course it is not just the relationship between the stars and the Earthly counterparts or communication network, but amongst members of those systems,the Star people and each other. So, the relationship between both those Star systems is that they are part of a mutual support system, not only those two but others also are related in the systems, not just in the pyramids and the chambers within the pyramids but also between the different pyramids themselves.It will come to pass sometime that the Scientists will begin to relate and report upon this themselves, as this era progresses so the interest will increase, the sensitivity of the measuring will increase and what has passed for magic will be proven scientifically.

The beings from Alnitak are very advanced and have colonies in other parts of the Cosmos. Other people go to their star system for learning, for they are teachers. They have not taught just on a celestial basis, a cosmic basis, but they have also been teachers upon the Earth plane in Ancient Times. But now, of course, part of that knowledge passed on because there is no need for them to visit, for you have amongst the earth people the genes of such people. The learning, which will be revealed, is being revealed at the present time in much the same way that you, in your heart of hearts, have a knowing that the Siriun people exist and that the Polarian people exist and so on. In the New Age more of this hidden knowledge is being revealed.

Pyramids, Ritual and the Ben-Ben Stone

KERRY

What is the purpose of the Ben-Ben stone, where did it come from and why?

AT-HLAN

The stone you refer to is meteoric in origin and it's purpose was originally to transmit power. For there were rituals carried out around this stone, it had inscriptions around it which were to do with both the ritual and the modern method of transmitting energy. When it was used under the proper circumstances it glowed with energy and could be seen from a great distance. It was a precursor, it came before the pyramids and there are several similar such monuments around the earth. They were made to communicate with particular stars, and this one itself, interestingly enough, was used to communicate with those star systems in the belt of Orion. But it would depend upon the time and the place, and there was much time given so that the declination was correct and that there was maximum communication sent out. But you see, even so there were limits on what could be communicated for you may go to a granite Menhir and put your hand on that stone, as some of you have done, and send out your thoughts. This is a simple form of some type of signalling "We are here, we send out Peace and Love to the Universe" were the sort of messages and also with the hope of Peace and Love being returned and bring health and harmony to those particular people, which is why many of these stones were erected. So you see, communication has been going on for thousands upon thousands of years at different levels. Some at a simple, primitive level and some at a more advanced level depending on the civilisations rise and fall and rise again. But as I have said, it seems that these forms of communication ceased to be used but the reasons are manifold.

It is clearer, more complex and more use when people such as yourselves sit and send out their own messages in a more complex way and begin to communicate with those that are a great distance away. Also to see the results of this communication, see that people from other parts of the galaxy may come and visit your circles without all the 'mumbo jumbo' and ritual that went with the sending of signals which became pointless rituals. For the real reasons got lost in the mists of time. We would say again that it is your clearer channels

without all the pomp and ceremony that are the future of communication for we
have found that people paint themselves and dress up in different garments and
cause pointless and senseless acts of destruction to be made in a cause that was
not there in the beginning. And so power against power comes in and this is
wrong, it will not be given the energies to proceed.

*There are many theories concerning the Ben-Ben stones; that they represented the
universe; that they were the cap stones of pyramids; that they were worshipped inside
the pyramids as the source of all life; that in the form of an obelisk they represented the
sun. At-Hlan discusses the original Ben-Ben stone almost as it were a gift from cosmic
beings, already inscribed, to help those upon the earth plane to continue their
communications with extra-terrestrial beings. When he states that it pre-dates the
Egyptian pyramids we wonder if it was given at that time and place when the Atlanteans
were beginning to establish a great 'new' colony in Egypt (?20,000BC) as it held
information and transferred energies communicating ideas and directions for the
construction of buildings, or was it brought with the Atlanteans.*

HANNAH
What was the purpose of the Sarcophagus, was it for initiation ceremonies?

AT-HLAN
Again you see the original sarcophagus, or sarcophagi, that you refer were used
in the pyramids as entrances and exits to different subterranean pathways. They
were indeed used in forms of initiation for self discipline of the mind, for
sensitization at many levels of being, but later they became places to bury
people, to put bodies in. But you see, there were thirteen different ways of
initiation, there were thirteen exits and entrances. The first initiation would be
to enter a particular portal to an experience and then exit at a different one,
sometimes through a sarcophagus. But sometimes as the initiate becomes more
wise, more informed, more knowledgeable, then they would go on to the second
and third and so on, the initiate would go on thirteen of these journeys. If you
wished to go on one of these journeys then you may do so in one of your circles
without any fear, for we would not wish to put you through the same mental
strain. But to perhaps experience it second hand, objectively, more as a tourist
than getting mentally involved, to see some of the trials, to sense some of the
ways of making the personal vibration of such a high vibration that things,
beings, sounds and senses could be sensed at a very great distance eventually.
But those people, those high initiates of the high times in the great cultures of

Egypt and Atlantis, had to leave a very careful life for they could be very easily unbalanced by sounds and by many colours and senses in their normal everyday life. The way that we progress in these days is much more down to Earth and although you mediums do become oversensitive, you find you can still be very sensitive in your mediumship without having to undergo the somewhat traumatic experiences of the initiation of 4000 or 5000 years ago.

HANNAH
What is the significance of the thirteen initiations?

AT-HLAN
I am told (*at this point At Hlan confers with his people*) that there are certain numbers that are supposedly magical in context, like the number twelve, as there are twelve months in the year, twelve disciples and so on, but the number thirteen relates to the direct number of influences, Star influences, upon the planet Earth. The influences upon the planet Earth are from thirteen different Star Systems and there was a knowledge one time of the precise star systems, and a good knowledge of the beings that inhabited those systems with whom there was communication. Not always clear communication for you must not assume that the Atlanteans and the Egyptians always knew precisely what they were doing in terms of communication. They did have a very sophisticated communication system with some of those star systems, but thirteen is the number that was found to have a more profound effect upon the beings who were upon the planet Earth. So in a way you are influenced to a larger or lesser degree by this one or that one. You see you have thirteen signs of the Zodiac cycle, so it almost goes back, not to a myth, but to a reality or close to a reality. In fact if you take the twelve star signs and you add the Sun then you have thirteen.

LENETTE
The Pyramid Scrolls that are about to be found, the ones I saw in meditation, what is the relevance of them to life today and are they Egyptian or Atlantean and are they anything to do with the work of Thoth?

148

AT-HLAN

You will find that some of those manuscripts do date from the Atlantean and later additions were made in the Egyptian era. In fact later you will find reference to Hermes Trismagistus also in there, who was a very wise person who was also related to the teachings of Thoth, but I would not like to take too much experience away from you. In your circle you will be given further instruction in how to translate and use these ancient tablets and writings that you have found. It is a very high teaching, not always relevant to todays society, it is interesting to them but not always relevant. But it does make reference in there to the great cataclysm that eventually was the downfall of the Atlantean society. You will find that not only have the intercontinental plates moved to bring that cataclysm about but also of the large meteor that impacted to cause the rift, to cause the volcanoes and the upsurge of energy that brought about the final demise of the Atlantean civilisation. But even so, this is a rather simplistic way of referring to the Atlanteans, for like all people then they had been the major force upon the Earth plane for tens of thousands of years and as you know made many colonies and transferred their culture to many parts of the Earth plane. So it was not the destruction of Atlantean genes but of the place where all the culture originated and all this you will find in those writings.

Star Influences and the Atlanteans

HANNAH
We have heard that there are three planets in the Siriun Solar system where people such as the Lion people and the Crystal people come from, could you give us more information on this please.

AT-HLAN
You would have to go more towards Alpha Centuri, where you have people who would appear to have an overall likeness towards those animals you call lions. They are not truly very similar at all, but their faces are rather feline. They have green eyes, irises which are both vertical and horizontal. They have a sandy covering to their bodies and fine hair. They do not have claws but have arms and legs and walk upright. They have quite large ears but they do not have tails. These are peoples towards Alpha Centuri. The Siriuns, from where Azgar and others come, indeed use crystals in many different ways not dissimilar to what was impressed upon the Atlanteans. They used crystals to store energy and to us it for building and time/space continuum. This enabled them to transport thoughts and images of themselves to communicate with other places in the Cosmos. Wavelengths of peace, harmony and love are sent out where it is necessary to distances that you would consider to be millions of light years away.

So these people have different reasons for their existence and have been linked in at different levels. These so called lion people have had the power of telepathic thought and appear to you as quite primitive people. They are not primitive, by no means, and they have a large capacity to think, to use logic, and to use philosophy at quite a deep level. Although they have not yet transported themselves physically from their planet they can send out thought photographs, thought images of themselves to certain people upon the Earth Plane. They are very soft and gentle, not ferocious at all. Of course their image has been picked up by some writers here, as in 'Narnia'. They are very gentle, light, careful and timid people, unlike Azgar who is not timid!

PATSY
The Lion People, were they people that influenced Egypt with some of their Gods?

AT-HLAN

I am empowered to say you have the Sphinx as a memory of this, and so on. Sometimes you are sent lions to come with your guides, some bring animals with them to represent power, not a power that is destructive but a thought power that is full of love, devotion and humility. In the early times of setting up of the colonies in Egypt indeed there were such people. These people could focus upon these and others across the Universe, who knew of their power, their influence and their direction. They had much to do with directing the thought of others should they so wish. They were used to direct and bring to a focus other influences as well. So, you have different peoples depicted in the hieroglyphics that the Egyptians were able to do. There were very highly developed mediums there, who did not deal so much in the early days with the world of spirit but with the cosmic influences there. You have got people with wolves heads on, the head of an Ibis and so on. These are different influences, not always accurately drawn but certainly drawn as the mediums saw them at that time. There were places where these people were welcomed and their knowledge was listened to by what you would call High Priests, the initiated, those wise ones who are also influenced by the White Brotherhood.

The Relationship Between Atlantis and Egypt

PATSY

We would like to know about the link between Atlantis, Peru and Egypt. I have some drawings that I am working on could you give us some information please?

AT-HLAN

Atlantis was in its prime for some three million years. During this time there were many sub races from that root race, from what are called Ramohals, Tvatlis, Semites and so on. There was a great cultural and spiritual development in Atlantis and in the places that it colonised for the right reasons. For it brought great, high and devout teachings to those places and influenced peoples, not through wars, but through wisdom. The mainland of the American Continent was part of the Atlantean Empire influences. You will find if you go back before the Olmecs to the Tlavatli then they are the descendants of the original Atlantean race. You have other races that were given powers and on the main continent of North and South America. From there they became the Aztecs and Incas, but the Aztecs, even before they had been conquered by the Spaniards, had perverted the Truths. They had come to a stage where they were about to destroy their own people by a heirachy of Priests and politicians who demanded great sacrifice upon sacrifice. The heart of the beings were taken, literally, on a self destructive pattern of ritual where the hearts were used to empower priesthood instead of direct relationship with the Great Mind, the human mind and the human heart. They were on a great downward spiral and had been so for many thousands of years.

If you look at the Inca, they had left at the stage between the Toltec and the Olmec to escape the brutality of the priesthood. They set up the colony that you know of in South America and for a long time there was peace and tranquillity. Even though they had leaders with great power the power was used to be shared equally among the people. Even so, the Incas made war on tribes, killing thousands of people, had it not been for the Spaniards they after a time would have destroyed themselves. Although on a positive side there are ancient wisdoms that live among sections of those people in their minds and in their histories. The great souls, those who walk in the light will of course incarnate

152

to other cultures where the Light and the Truth will shine again and has shone again. It does so upon this area of the Earth among you, which is why you are able to do your drawings and why your interest in such things has been stimulated. You see it brings me back to my point that you have lived in many lives and upon many planes of existence.

At-Hlan begins to focus upon the links and lineage of different races and cultures and draws our attention to the misuse of power, the perversions of Truth, the opportunities we have had for advancement and thrown it away. But there is an overall plan, reasons for our existence and an increasing awareness, at this present time, in our evolution, that we must take hold of our responsibilities, our freedom of choice, and begin to share the light of Universal love with our brothers and sisters here on earth and with those upon different planes of existence.

HANNAH
There seems to be quite an increase on the connection with Egypt- The Pyramid journeys, Patsy's drawings etc. Could you tell us why Egypt is so relevant to us at the moment?

AT-HLAN
Yes, because there is in some ways a similar vibration upon the Earth plane at the moment as there was 15,000-12,000 B.C. and 3,000 to 2,000 BC, and a similar vibration as 500 BC. There are increased electro magnetic forces upon this particular cycle of the Earth Plane, which is brought by the Cosmic Masters but also links it in with Gaia Tellus, the Earth Mother. So we match our vibrations to help to move the evolution of mankind and the human soul forward somewhat.

In some ways the Spiritual level of that time in Egypt and the level at the present times is similar. It is very easy for you to,link back with Egypt because of the similarity in vibration.You can cross the time and space' continuum very, very easily, if there is an upward circle, a spiral going up and here you may reach down to a previous and similar time upon that spiral. It is very easy to make those links and of course when you have made those links you begin to realise that you yourselves have had an incarnation at that time. That is another part of the jigsaw. If you had not had incarnations then you could not make the links, and so on and so forth. Basically that is the reason why, of course there are differences, the world has progressed in some ways and regressed in others. You will make your links with the Cosmos, you will realise that you are of Star stuff, that you have had incarnations on other planets. Not through ritual, but through that inner knowing, for as I have said many of you have progressed beyond the Egyptian era.

The Egyptians, and before them, the Atlanteans, built these monuments to help channel these energies. There was much good work done through these monuments in the way they were built and the types of energies that they linked in to. You do not need monuments or buildings, you need people who were warm hearted, full of love, clear minded and open to allow further awareness to expand their minds, to expand their memories, to allow them to realise that the past, present and future co-exist.

Akhenaton and Khufu

PATSY

Why is Akhenaton, out of all the Pharaoh's in Egypt, the one who seems to be the most important to our circle.?

AT-HLAN

We would not say that he is the most important one. Certainly, Menes was important, Khufu was important. Akhenaton arrived, as it were, at a time with so much Cosmic energy and insight. He arrived at a time, when like the person, the master Jesus, when there was a downturn in the cultural state of Egypt, as there was a downturn in the cultural state of what you would call the middle Eastern countries. Akhenaton, in spirit, arrived there to try to bring back the spirituality to that culture, for it had diverted from the pathway of Truth and enlightenment into some small sub-culture. Some of whom were working at a psychic level, some were working at discontent, working for the left hand path, working in a way that was parallel to the downfall of the Atlantean culture. Akhenaton came to re-state that power was not to be misused, that it must not be used to wage war against people, to bring disease and distruction. It must be used to bring forward the progression of all mankind.

You see, at that time the Pharaoh's sycophantic elite began to separate themselves from the people. They used the power for their own progression, so they thought, of course without using spiritual insight and knowledge for all the people. Akenaton came to bring back the power of the Solar Logos of the Great Spirit that organises and controls the planetary system. This helps to make communication between that system and other parts of the galaxy and the Universe in general, and he came to shine the Light, to bring all of the people back to learning, knowledge and wisdom and to set up the libraries. Akhenaton was overthrown by the displaced peoples, the people who would wage warfare. He was most cruelly destroyed through torture and adverse powers that destroyed his earthly brain. You see you cannot destroy a great spirit and a Cosmic Master, for you are now tuned in to a facet of the wisdom and sage like qualities of the Master.

PATSY

You mentioned Khufu and Menes. As you know, I have drawn a picture of Khufu. There is really nothing I can find to read about him.. could you give us some information please.

AT-HLAN

My channel was talking about being 'low profile' about an hour ago, was he not, Khufu is a shortened name of that entity who was surrounded, as you would say, in the magical mists of time. Who was an Avatar, who protected himself from adverse influences and worked quietly here and there. Infact, he could project himself over great distances whilst being in one place. He could simultaneously transfer himself to many places, as in fact you do when you are linked into the network of thought transference. You may take part of your energy and be an influence a great distance away from your body, as all of you should understand. It is part of your work that you do when you send out thoughts. At that level you become part of someone elses life and an influence perhaps hundreds or thousands of miles away. There would not have been much written or graphically detailed about this entity . Having known the misuse of power, again, this was a higher evolved soul who came to bring peace and harmony.

He was a soul who helped link the two tribes of Egypt, the Upper and Lower parts of Egypt. He could be in Heliopolos and Alexandria simultaneously, and at Memphis and so on. The work that went on was one of great forces of the Earth Mother, the Spiritual and Cosmic forces. Much work was done in building a special monument and much of that was secret and hidden from the eyes of mankind so that it could not be misused. That power still is there, in Egypt, and we see the Light shining from that special place where the magnetic lines of the Earth cross most strongly. Not always do you need the presence of man in the physical but this is visited by those from the spiritual and cosmic worlds. Although I say 'spirit and cosmic', of course at a certain level one becomes the other as it were and both combine to do both kinds of work, spiritual work for the Earth Mother that links automatically with the cosmic experiences of these people. I have had to rely on my other informants more strongly in answer to that question because some information is given to me that either is beyond my recall or has been outside of my terms of reference. Now I also have that knowledge, so you see we all learn together sometimes.

Learning is definitely not only a one-way system, for as we progress we exchange information, at a super-conscious level, with our guides and as we appear to have an excess of the energy of love, which, when used in the appropriate manner, empowers the guides and high spiritual and cosmic beings and so not only do they rejoice but are similarly uplifted as we are. We are all part of a network of light and if we choose to add our energies then we positively feel the feed-back in being more aware of influences in our own lives (which helps us 'take charge' of our lives) and our guides get 'promoted', if you like, for they have helped to guide, counsel and influence more people or beings and so more responsibility is given to them - as it is to us.

The Downfall of Atlantis

DEBBIE

Some scientists have found under the Atlantic Ocean a plateau called telegraph plateau. It has mountains on it all covered in volcanic mass - is this Atlantis?

AT-HLAN

I must explain to you first of all, the concept of Atlantis and Lemuria which was before it. You see the evolution of the earth goes back many millions of years with races that have reached a low state of evolution and others that have reached a high state, particularly on the spiritual plane. Your world 'scientifically', in a material sense, has reached a very high state but not so spiritually. The soul Atlantis may go back for several million years and there have been changes in the geographical structure after the event of Lemuria, before Atlantis and several times during the Atlantis period, in which there were many different races evolved to bring different work at a different level upon the earth plane. So that plateau to which you refer and the surrounding area has been elevated above the waters of the earth at some stage and there will be scientific proof of buildings and of instruments that were linked with the star systems and of vast distances which will amaze the scientists because there were only primitive men like Neanderthal men existing in the earth plane. You see while these people existed there were other higher and sometimes hidden races and sub races that reached at the same time a very high standard of spiritual knowledge and energy.

HANNAH

Is the Bermuda Triangle anything to do with Atlantis, if so where have all the ships and planes gone?

AT-HLAN

Well you see when the Atlanteans built their cities there were various sorts of metals used and it was built in that particular place because it was what you would say today, 'the crossing of many ley lines', a magnetic centre, which is why Poseidonis was built the way it was built, the Golden City. There are still energies in that area that have effect on the steering of ships and the navigation of flying machines. Some of them seem to have drifted towards the Sargasso

Sea where they have become entangled with the great sea of seaweed that is found in that place. They have not magically disappeared or teleported to a distant planet or apported to another place.

KERRY

Will some of the continent of Atlantis ever emerge as proof of it's existence?

AT-HLAN

Well, it has been said by some fortune tellers and forecasters that Atlantis will emerge again, and so it is emerging again. When we remember that you are all Star Seeds and your ways of communication can bring that to the fore as well as your memories and journeys to and from Atlantis, so Atlantis in the memory of people is becoming clearer and clearer. So you have reached a stage whereby people less frequently scoff and deride the idea of the Atlantean civilisation because it is being revealed in their heart of hearts that that is so. So, Atlantis in that sense is symbolically re-emerging. But time goes on in this planetary system in a particular way, your peoples will find more and more evidence that there are subterranean buildings, they will find parts of the culture of the Temples, of the statues and even the watertight boxes in which there are evidence of writings to be found. But the idea that Atlantis will slowly pop up again in the middle of the ocean is stretching the capabilities a little too far, don't you think! (*laughter*).

KERRY

Exactly where was it that Atlantis was supposed to have sunk, It's all new to me as well. I always believed that Atlantis was fiction so I would like to know for myself?

AT-HLAN

It is where these books have said, in the Atlantic Ocean off the coast of North America. As those maps that my channel has in the room show you, they are precisely where the maps say they were because those maps were drawn through Cosmic inspiration, to show people that Atlantis was not just a small Island that suddenly sank in the sea. Over hundreds of thousands if not millions of years the surface of the planet changes and so different cultures come and go, but always there is an upward spiral, always there are challenges. But we feel that despite hypocrisy and perversions of Truths, that we are beginning on an era where Universal Truth, Universal Knowledge is being used once again to bring what you would call, your civilisations, into closer contact with what the Greeks and the Romans called the Gods. For indeed in one sense there is more than one God, for the Great Mind has many messengers as all the Ancient Civilisations showed in different forms like Isis, Osiris and so on. So you are beginning to contact the Higher Teachers, the Sanat Kumara, because we Masters are very pleased to be part of this communication network where the Light begins to shine in various places.

PATSY

I have a question from a friend of ours called Richard. The question is, and these are his exact words, "What is under the South China Sea between the Phillipines and Hong Kong?"

AT-HLAN

Yes, we know of Richard. We will confer... These are some of the remnants of Ancient Lemurian civilisations that pre-date Atlantis. He is indeed right. They, in their temples, used many different kinds of crystals for communication network. For these are buried at quite a deep level when the larger Islands sank beneath the sea it took with it quite a primitive peoples in some ways, but again, they were very good at communication. We can see quite large crystals, purple and green were used quite a lot, but we could go into much detail to say specifically how these purple and green were used for one reason and then there were red and yellow used for another. But they are buried quite a way below what you would call mud deposits, from what you would call anti-deluvian slime, from volcanoes, from the ash and the outpourings from those volcanoes in that area. These were a yellow people, quite small in stature by your standards, about 4' high, who inhabited this area, who did not grow to a great culture so far as high buildings were concerned, but as a simple culture they were very good communicators in terms of being able to be telepathic. They did this by being able to use the vibrations of the stones and crystals to help this communication pattern between themselves and sometimes between certain temples they had and cosmic influences also, even if you go back for 5 million years this was so.

PATSY

Thank you At-Hlan, I will pass that information on to Richard.

DEBRA

Is it true that when Atlantis fell, some of them were able to come away and get to England?

AT-HLAN

Atlantis was a big island in the Atlantic, we would say about the third of the size of Australia, it was in total -what you would say goes back to about 130,000 years B.C. There was a cataclysm which split Atlantis into two islands, and a third cataclysm which happened about 12,000 years ago, which divided Atlantis into many islands. You must realise that by this time we had colonised various parts of the world as it was then. If you wanted to trace the facts of this, you could go to Egypt where you would find that there was no ancient civilisation. The colony of Atlantis, which started with a very high civilisation with all of the home civilisation - the home city - could provide. We worked with crystals, with clairvoyance, with flying machines but at this highest point of development there was no pollution of the Earth, it was all done by what you might call a natural science. Has this answered your questions?

DEBRA

Yes, but when the cataclysms occurred, there was a story that this was brought on by the evil of the people there, which made it happen.

AT-HLAN

This is correct. The original inhabitants of Atlantis, were from other worlds. They were in spirit form combined with people through various means, were more earth bound, but yes, of a spiritual civilisation. Some of the priests - remember that this is after tens of thousands of years - turned the high vibration to become self-centred, and to bring it down to the most basic feelings of the animal level, and it became a perversion of the spiritual values when the Gods were formed -not the true Gods - and sacrifices were performed. There were warnings from the Gods thorough their priests, that there would be catastrophes. These warnings were ignored and so that was eventually the collapse of the system in Atlantis.

In this earlier channeling (1992) there was much interest shown in the story of Atlantis, before our thoughts were directed towards cosmic communications, and so this particular information was rather confusing until later when we were informed more fully of the evolutionary cycle and the different extra-terrestrial influences brought to bear upon our progression.

SYBIL
May I ask if I actually go back to Atlantis?

AT-HLAN
Yes, this is true. At this time and for some time. You will read with the writer Edgar Cayce that there are many Atlantians becoming incarnated on the Earth Plane for a purpose, because we are of the Aquarian age. We are in the process of moving the spiritual evolution forward for many people. This is an area which is very highly protected by the Great Spirits - by the Super Astral Plane, and it is important that you have the knowledge and the purity to know and not to be afraid.

DAVE
How did pyramid power play a large role in Atlantis? This is shown in places like Egypt, where there is great power.

AT-HLAN
You will find that the pyramids are in seven areas of the world. This was a structure not just to channel the energy, which it did, but it was a living temple as were the pyramids in Egypt which was initiated. This is where they had their direction. By this I mean that we could fortell what would happen and to some extent prevent the collapse, for example, of the Egyptian Empire, because there were leaders who were priests, and there were warrior priests. I myself, was a warrior priest. My channel here is Rohann, who, as an Atlantean, knew of this system.

PATSY
You mentioned the other week a planet called Tellemarkus and you said it would be homework for us to do. Well we have tried to find it but we cannot, so we are hoping that you can enlighten us.

AT-HLAN
Well, I could do to a degree but I do not like to do all the work for you. It was

in ancient times - the twin influence of Castor and Pollux - those two star systems, and they were seen as the twin energies and the legs of a great being. You will find that great being in Greek mythology if you look there. Simple and straight-forward!

Telemachus was Odysseus's son who waited patiently for his father's return and who became the sole supporter of Odysseus's plan to prove who he was. Telemachus was convinced of his father's identity (disguised as an old man) when an old staghound they used to hunt with recognised Odysseus as his master. Odysseus, after overthrowing the opposition, then became happily reunited with his son and his wife Penelope, and from this we may happily deduce many things. Firstly, and most obviously, that the influence of Castor and Pollux is important, secondly we may look to the dog-star Polaris as an important piece of the puzzle and, thirdly, perhaps we have to be as observant as Telemachus and as patient as Penelope who undid at night the work she did by day, to gain time. At-Hlan seems to be gaining time and having a joke at our expense.

Humorous Aspects of Universal Knowledge

HANNAH
A most serious question At-Hlan.. we think that as part of our studies we ought to visit Egypt. Can you arrange this for us please and thank you!!!

AT-HLAN (Laughs)...
You have already visited Egypt several times and it is not difficult as you know. But it is nice in a way to have the humour and nice to know that other people would like to come if they had the open channel with it. You must remember that you are brought into a circle because you have that open channel, and for some, who have work in different areas, they do not always have the capability or the facilities to do this. But we would bring you facts that although you appear to travel back in time thousands of years, or you appear to travel forwards in time thousands of millions of years, it is all in the present and the present, past and future are all one. So it is not difficult for you to both visualise, sense and see your past, present and future, for you have already travelled faster than light to planetary systems. You have gone back in what you consider to be time, but it is really not so, all exist at the same place, the place within you, rather than any historic time of the future or the past. That is quite difficult to explain...When you tune into Universal Knowledge you have access to that knowledge instantaneously, and so, past and future do not exist, and in a sense the present does not exist either,it is only your wisdom, your learning, your higher self that exists.

KERRY
So does that mean yes?! (*Loads of laughter!*)

AT-HLAN
You will travel 1st Class when ever you have many challenges, when you have travelled further along the pathway, when you have opened more and more doors, when you have access to closer knowledge from the Great Being, from the systems that eminate from the Great Being who you call God. Then you may travel 1st Class! Of course you would always give up your seat to somebody else who was in more need of it than yourself. That is the sign that you have indeed travelled a great distance, to turn back from the final journey and allow

others to go before you.

We could go on adding to this information 'Ad Infinitum', but to give too much would not be understood and so we stop where we are about to begin, so that where we have stopped in the future other people may ask further questions and so expand the knowledge of this wonderful Universe we all inhabit, at whatever level or stage of development we are. You have done well this afternoon. I thank you for your company and your questions and your humour. I leave you all with my love and my peace.

As At-Hlan became accustomed to members of the circle, and vice-versa, so some questions became light-hearted and At-Hlan has added to or joined in the humour but, as is seen from the two example above, he then continues with a serious interpretation of the questions. He is insistent that if we attune ourselves with truth and commitment, under the correct circumstances, and conjure the correct atmosphere then we may tap into aspects of Universal Consciousness where 'all is known' relevant to our enquiries. There are constraints, though, for we must be at the level of development to understand the knowledge given for the right reasons and it must not break the code of the Divine Plan. At-Hlan insists that the past, present and future co-exist if we look in the right direction, follow the appropriate pathway and therefore experience that plane of existence which is certainly beyond the linear concepts we adhere to in the third dimension.

Chapter 8   ***Our Place in the Universe***

Contents   Humans as Cosmic Beings

Of U.F.O.s and All That

The Jupiter Effect

Black Holes and the Space-Time Continuum

De-atomisation, Astral and Telepathic Journeying

The Relationship of Star Systems with Individuals
and Planet Earth

166

Humans as Cosmic Beings

KERRY
I have heard it said that planets and stars in certain positions on the time and day you were born go on to affect the rest of your life. Is this so?

AT-HLAN
Of course everything works on vibrations, there are vibrations and influences all the time, given that you are born at a certain time, it is important it is related back to the time of your conception and forward to the rest of the time of your life, but this does not take away your own personal choices. It does mean to say that certain planets and stars will have an influence in the rythms and patterns of your life, but this also fits into a network to produce positive influences in your life. Often there have to be adverse influences, something that you have to battle against, and so there is a soul growth and when the soul grows then the adverse influences lessen. Always there will be choices there and as you take on more responsibility in your life as you are doing, all of you, then so those decisions are made at a higher level. Refuse that responsibility then, in a sense, the Angels cry, because the influences have worked together to help you shine that light, to help you send out clear thoughts of Truth and Commitment and if the wrong pathway is followed then you have refused your responsibilities. So, you have to face responsibilities some time in the future.

So the answer to your question is - Yes! Also I will add something to that; for those of you who have had many cosmic influences which sometimes are not shown perhaps on your Astrological chart, then there is also an invisible influence there. Whenever you have had contact with other people, other conditions, that influence is always there with you. That is why it always gives us great pleasure to bring the cosmic influences into focus on the Earth plane. So you see , as the brother Jonathan has said, he has had a Siriun incarnation, which is absolutely correct. Sometimes people do not incarnate for a period of time on the Earth plane, they are off experiencing something that is there so the network builds up on a multi-dimensional level.

Of U.F.O.s and All That

PATSY

I would like to ask a question about cosmic beings and the relevance of them coming in their physical forms , in the forms of U.F.O's and as well as their spiritual forms if indeed the two are connected.

AT-HLAN

When you perceive, when you are perceptive to those beings such as Azgar and Zargon and others in your circle, it is a telepathic link - it is the essences of that person ,their background and culture, how they think and to a large degree how they look. Even though the names are nominal so that you may recognise them for their own vibration. It may be unrecognisable and in some cases beyond your auditory system to be able to hear. So they project themselves with the energies you send, with the love vibration, the commitment to truth as they have done for tens of thousands of years. In fact the beings who use space vehicles come physically to explore the earth fields for you have attracted beings from many differernt parts of the galaxy, not only with thought but with your telecommunication instruments.

Some of these influences are here just to explore and investigate and add you to the list of peoples that they know on different planets. Different life forms come for the wrong reasons, they are out of time, they misuse their knowledge to make explorations of the physical bodies of people on the earth plane. One of these people come from the Pleiades. They physically transport faster than light speed, in some cases many times faster for they have the information of space/time continuum and can project themselves faster than you can see which is why if you look at the source of light generated by the flying machine sometimes they appear to disappear for they have gone very quickly indeed. We in some ways do not approve of these visitations, however delightful and significant they may seem to you, for we do not wish the evolutionary cycle of beings upon the earth to be interfered with in any direct way, even though we are always here to help and assist those who would walk along the pathway of wisdom. So there are several battles in a way, there are several thought systems which are fighting against each other to ensure the evolution continues as it should without direct interference.

Most of the people who visit the earth plane would wish to do so incognito, but your technology has increased very much, very quickly during the last thirty or so of your years. So this has been upsetting those powers that have made contact with these space machines many, many, times. But of course they do not inform the ordinary people in case there is hysteria or panic. Even the friendly peoples who visit there wish to remain incognito, and where you have imprints in your plants, the so called corn circles, these are friendly messages to say that there are other beings who visit you, and yet it is a matter of discussion whether it is a good or a bad thing. You see, we wish to make contact, but we wish the contact to be smooth and based on understanding. This is a problem at many different levels for many different beings.

MARY
From time to time we read in our newspapers that people meet up with so called aliens and are taken up into space ships and experiments are performed on them which appear not to be very pleasant. Can you explain if this is correct?

AT-HLAN
There are always two sides of a coin, there is always evil where there is good, positivity where there is negativity and this brings about progression. If there is an imbalance it brings about a darker side of life and there are vibrations which are destructive. All life wherever you are is based on this equation. So there are entities like Azgar and Zargon, somebody who is yet to channel for you and with you, who comes with the light and there are others from the darker side who bring their machines for the purpose of reversing the progression of the human soul. It is not as has been said to experiment with fertility with a view to populating or colonising this planet, for those beings would not be capable of doing so under their conditions, but interrupt, to pervert the course of light. The governments on the other planes know of their existence and are confused as to why they have come here but there are several people from the 'dark side of the moon' is the way to explain it, that come for the wrong reasons and to take that which is not theirs and not theirs to own.

ANNE
U.F.O.'s and extra-terrestrials, they are advanced civilisations supposed to be helping the world so why is it that we hear of people being kidnapped, tortured and even disappear?

170

AT-HLAN

Well, this is food for thought. You see the most advanced beings do not need transportation by U.F.O's , there are those who come to this planet out of genuine interest because they have reached a stage in their evolution where this has just become possible. Several cultures or civilisations, one of which seems to adversely affect you is in fact from the Seven Sisters, the Pleiades, most of them genuinely wish to find out more and so you find as you refer to those kidnappings going on, this is against Universal Law. Their advancement in their own planetary system will stultify because they have misused their power. There are also those who can use Light Machines, as I call them, because they are not really Flying Saucers, although they may appear in this shape. Sometimes they appear round or cylindrical, but it is the emanations that give it this effect. Others come not to investigate, but to send out signals in their way to help, to assist and sometimes to warn as well as to care and protect. There are different beings for different reasons. It is supreme irony that in many ways you cannot progress without having seen both the Light and the Dark. Even on a Cosmic scale there are difficulties, but from these difficulties and adverse influences grows the Light. There are thought forms and energies produced from the conflict between the Light and the Dark. The Great Mind always knows and understands the struggles both at a cosmic level and an individual level.

LENETTE

Do stars that have died, if they have influenced us when they were here, have a detrimental effect when they go?

AT-HLAN

When star systems are made the energy is given to them for a purpose and the purpose has been written many times in what has been said before hand, but it has given an energy and a life to combine with planets and other star systems and for the progression of other beings and send signals of various and quite complex nature. On some planets there is an evolution of a life form, sometimes visible, often invisible ,to your eyes. When these systems of evolution have ceased then the energy is taken from that system and is recycled, you might say, and planned into the network of amother place. Remember the scientists saying there is a reaction and that energies that are used never just disappear they are just passed on to be used in another place. So it is a very well organised system where that energy is reused wherever necessary in that part of the cosmos.

PATSY

Going back to the cosmic influences what extra terrestrial powers influence the Earth most at the present?

AT-HLAN

Well I have already mentioned the systems of Sirius, Polaris and Aldebaran Vega and also of course you have the Pleiades with your pieces of rock from there (moldavite). It is a future influence in a way, although its presence is just being felt for the moment, for there are interesting and in some cases parallel evolutionary cycles going on in the system of the universe. Also it has been said earlier that the scientists will find very old stars and very young stars, many young stars in that system and although it is before the time of the planets - although cycles, in some terms of space and time, came into existence after the earth cycle as it were - it has many old stars and many young stars, so that will be interesting for the scientists to probe because there are always old and new influences. Indeed, in a way how can there be new influences without the older influences there to help the cycles, to give out information, to help the organisation of the new - it is rather like having a young child and a knowledgeable elder parent or grandparent to help when it came into being and to help it find its way in that particular system and how it relates to other systems as well.

PATSY

Can you tell us a little bit more about the stone Moldavite, why is it so special?

AT-HLAN

My channel has begun to probe the different areas of existence. We said earlier that the influence of the Pleiades is beginning to be felt upon the Earth plane and Moldavite was sent to help the progress, to focus the spiritual forces, to help give awareness of the positive virtues. You notice that the stone is green which is for growth, which is for positive emotions. It has many connotations among mankind. Indeed there is a cup, a chalice that you call the Holy Grail, there is such a cup. It has such a green stone in it which is in an unseen place in a museum in Cairo and nobody knows why it is there and I am not about to divulge why! But there is such a cup there which is gathering the dust, but it has other stones as well set into that Golden chalice.

So, Moldavite has been sent, as have other meteorites that extra-terrestrials have influenced, to help with the pattern and progress of mankind. But it was supposed to be to help in the sense that the Lady Hannah has spoken of, to reach the vibration within individuals, but not just in individuals but to be passed on once it has been used and polished and shaped, or in it's original state, to be passed from one to the other so that knowledge and harmony may spread. It has a very harmonising influence at a cosmic rather than a spiritual level. It is interesting also that many different stones have been made from the Earth's core, or sent from other places for different reasons, all of them good. But then again we can have a perversion of their mis-use, of the stone such as the diamond, when people have killed and have brought about bloodshed, envy and jealousy and this is a mis-use of the stone. So the power of the diamond has now been removed and diamonds are powerless to influence positively as they were being used to influence negatively.

The Jupiter Effect

LENETTE
Greetings At-Hlan, can tell us what effect the comet colliding with Jupiter will have on our planet?

AT-HLAN
Very little on a physical level, because due to the size of Jupiter and the smallness of this meteorite in comparison, and due to the atmosphere on Jupiter, it will be slow until it hits the core, as it were. But, cosmically it will have a different effect because there will be a signal that is sent out that will be relayed to the Earth. A signal concerning the fragility of the Earth and its relationship with the cosmos. Also it will be a reminder that at one level of the catastrophies that have happened upon the planet Earth, although it is not recorded in many books, of the meteor that was brought to the Earth to bring about the increased vibration or the rotation of the Earth at the end of the Atlantean period. The entities upon Jupiter are aware of this fact.

It will effect their planet to the extent that it will change the vibration of that planet to an infinitesimal amount and therefore it will sing a slightly different note which of course will effect all the other planets in the solar system. An infinitesimal amount is a very small amount and therefore it will be recognised still as the same planet and there will be a minimal effect certainly very little effect on the physical Mother Earth. It may bring back on the cosmic level one or two memories that will help to jar the focus of those people who are having difficulty in breaking through the time /space barrier, as it were, that you have broken through with your contacts with Polaris, Sirius and so on. (I have taken a long time for other entities have been communicating with me - so I hope it still makes sense). So it will be in a sense beneficial, in a sense that other peoples upon the earth will be able to recollect, if you like ,their cosmic past, their cosmic memory, the significance of extra terrestrial influences upon the earth plane. So this is part of the scheme of things to enlighten the higher souls upon the earth plane ,to jar the memory somewhat, to link in with what has been past so that the present maybe built upon ,which of course will alter the future. You will find that in the next 15-20 years there will be another phemomena that will be recorded by the scientists around the world which will make more feasible the connections that the earth plane has with the outer planets and with the other stars that influence the earth. So that the dates I have given you of 2012-2016 will be a combination of these different influences.

Perhaps the huge, mountains of material hurled at jupiter have had some influence in changing the electro-magnetic field of the earth. Some months after this information was received both At-Hlan and a guide through another member stated that due to the material purposefully guided to Jupiter it would effect the magnetic field of earth in such a way as to open the minds of many more people empowering them to become aware of the cosmic planes of existence.

LENETTE
Is this cosmic influence going to be more widespread, are we going to see an increase?

AT-HLAN
You see it has increased remarkably in the last decade the last twenty to thirty years it is a stronger influence in this stage of the earth's evolution and it will be remarkable to those people of a particular religious persuasion or faith that, apparently outside of their control or command ,so many people become involved in cosmic awareness, as the Great Mind is a super cosmic master as it were. Then to us this makes sense for your spirits do not come from the earth but from the Cosmos, which is common sense is it not? For the Spiritual Creator does not reside upon the planet earth but in the centre of creation for he is the creator. So it will change the philosophical climate upon the earth, as it will build if you take yourself as someone who has Truth on their side, of cosmic beings and influences you have found in your life and in your lives, that you have touched a soul here and another there and you have been quite surprised at the response and also at the knowledge that is being spread throughout the world, throughout many souls.

Despite some areas being dogmatic in belief there is a rising tide of awareness of the evolution of the human soul, of Gaia. Mother Earth is inextricably linked to the planetary system and to other influences, the influences of the stars and the star people, and it is important that at this point in the Earths time that this new Truth be expanded and expounded for without this there may well be a temporary regressive pathway which will become more and more introvert where religion and politics become more nationalistic, more destructive with this influence. People begin to look outside rather than inside of themselves and in that way there is the pathway of progression and understanding. So tied with this also is the expanded knowledge of the scientists who have quite a supportive role to play and some of them at this moment recognise that. So with this forward and outward looking dimension it should be unstoppable so that human beings and their souls see that they are not just earth people but star people and so they look outward and realise the stupidity of killing bodies, of torturing people, of waging war and so they will see themselves in a better perspective and a finer light eventually.

Black Holes and the Space-Time Continuum

TINA
What is in the Black Hole in space, and also is there anything beyond space?

AT-HLAN
If I were to explain the multi-faceted universe you would not understand, but let me try to explain that there is more than one universe. You only see at the present with your state of science, one dimension but there are many dimensions of the universe. When you realise that time and space do not exist as such, this is man made and you may travel the universe in the twinkling of an eye. Parts of the universe are in a state of imbalance, other parts of the universe are in various stages of development where there can be - what you would call a time space warp - where things are also reborn, where other aspects are completely made invisible or null and void or disappear completely because this is all part of the balance of harmony and disharmony of which you are part.

We would probably not have understood the full meaning at the time of this early session, for we were neither focussed in our thinking nor had we received the vast amount of extra-terrestrial information that pulled us along and gave us direction. As we grew in knowledge so we sensed At-Hlan's reasons for channeling and so he cleverly revealed more in-depth esoteric knowledge at the right stage in our development, some of which might have been completely misunderstood and therefore rejected out of hand. We still have a long way to go, as the following questions reveal!

HELEN
I was reading about the discovery of long wave and F.M. etc. If a radio can pick that up obviously then we are picking up your vibrations so that we can communicate with you. What exists between long wave and your communication and is there a machine that man can build to tune into them?

AT-HLAN
There are different levels and different channels of communication. Some of these channels of communication maybe local, some of them may extend again instantaneously through what we must refer to as time and space to other parts of the Galaxy. The work that you are concerned with involves both the psychosphere of the earth and the psychodynamics of the earth, which works

through electro-magnetic currents. Tuning into this, if you could visualise it is I can, there would be positive and negative influences, but all will be at different levels at different intensity at different channels. There is a whole network of different avenues surrounding not only the Earth, if you could look at a map you would see so many other influences from far and near as well brought about by different entities by spiritual and cosmic.

SALLY
Can you please define dimensions.

AT-HLAN
I will start by saying it is almost impossible to define dimensions but I will do my best. I am not saying that because I try to diminish you or your question but because it is a very complex area. Everything works at a vibration at a vibrational level. You work at a vibrational level as does the Mother Earth, the soul, the sun and so on. They have their existence at that level which is sometimes to do with the electrons, neutrons and so on which makes up that being. Also given off that being will be that note and so they are seen and perceived in that way. With that note comes colour or a mixture of colour as well. When a being from a different cosmic source perceives you it will be very rarely that they perceive your flesh but rather the vibration of that the way your body if you like, works upon this dimension. You are a being who works at a vibration on this dimension on the vibration of the Mother Earth.

The Mother Earth herself is influenced by other planetary systems and so there is a great network between you and your environment and your environment and other environments. A cosmic being may see you as colour, may see you just as a vibration or sense you as a vibration depending upon how they bring their own being here. The dimensions that you also refer to, the spiritual, the cosmic and so on are perhaps a little easier to explain. As you progress on the spiritual dimension there is a finer vibration and so gradually you inherit a different body, a different sound. You sound a different note, you become in a sense a finer person, you ascend to a different realm of being and you perceive different time and space. This is because you become involved in a different dimension. That is the closest I may get to explaining.

DEBRA

Is there a parallel Universe, is there such thing as anti-matter and would there be a problem if they met?

AT-HLAN

Let us take the first question. There are universes that operate on different vibrations, so this becomes complicated for man created for his own use, time and space. So, I will have to refer to those, though in a sense they do not exist at this vibration. If you could view this galaxy at different levels of vibration, you would see, not the planets that you see at the moment, but many other different planets that appear to you invisible but are just as realistically and tangibly there as Saturn or Jupiter, or Pluto, or Sirius for that matter. So, if you like, there are parallel Universes.

DEBRA

What about the question of anti-matter?

AT-HLAN

There are different forms of matter, as I have said of time and space. If there were a way in which some of these forms of matter could contact each other there would be vast imbalances, explosions, turbulences, but this is not the case, because they are held in a different dimension altogether where they are not allowed to meet. If you were taught about this phenomena, the Black Hole, then you would find that time and space alter differently and if you could look through those eyes you would not see planets just disappearing, but the life of new planetary systems and in fact, new forms of energy, being formed.

De-atomisation, Astral and Telepathic Journeying

SYBIL
Could I ask when de-atomization is likely to occur?

AT-HLAN
It is possible, as has been said, for some entities who have links with this planet from tens of hundreds or even thousands of light years away to be able to send themselves through the various ethers, so that in essence they become a presence in your circle as you have seen with Azgar, it is done in the twinkling of an eye and it is done through a particular high frequency or wave-length. This is what you might call de-materialization' or 're-materialization', or de-atomization or re-atomization in a similar way as in the past our thoughts have been sent and found, do you see?. It is possible in some degree for you to participate in this when you have the ability to send your etheric or astral body out into the world so that you may appear in Australia while your body is here. If this is done in a finely tuned way with your super-conscious mind fully alert you may bring back with you very clear thoughts of the senses and smells and experiences of that place or even what people have said you may even do, such as becoming a channel for healing. This is a very real thing to do and it is done for a proper reason in that case. The de-atomization of entities will happen, (I must re-phrase that), of human beings as it were, for this is how you originally phrased it, is possible at the moment at that level, the de-atomization of the physical body will become possible when there is enough power in circles and between circles so that at first you will send you finely attuned body and then you may be able to find that you can de-atomize your flesh and body, but of course this would take so much protection and under much secret and hidden and esoteric conditions that it is not likely that many people would have realisation of this.

DOROTHY
What we do now when we travel in the work that we do when we travel abroad to someone in distress, we look at our body and there isn't a body there but it is still felt, is this what you would class as de-atomization and once we can talk to the body in another land.?

AT-HLAN

I think you are referring here to sending your Astral body to another place where you may hear someone speak, you may sense their etheric body certainly and you may heal that body, which is of course to do with soul healing. You may get your super-conscious mind attuned with their super-conscious mind in close proximity so that the two are in communication and also overlap. It is also possible of course for you to effect their etheric aura so that you may balance that way, so there are different and complex ways in which you may effect this healing process and if it is done in such fine attunement it will alter their way of life and because you have influenced the soul, which influences other bodies, which influences the physical body and so the soul has been altered and what you might call the etheric body has been altered.

KERRY

Some planes of existence do not seem to have humour and yet it is what some beings are attracted to us by. How could there be such immense love with them but yet not humour because for us the two go hand in hand.

AT-HLAN

You see upon this particular planet there are so many aspects and facets of what I will term emotion. It can be the highest forms of love and the most negative forms of decadence or bestial behaviour, either positive and progressive or negative and destructive, that is the choice. So if we look at the various facets of this highly polished jewel called love one of the great linking networks is humour. It is if you like a sub-division or a slightly different vibration. It is being used to a great degree upon the earth plane. Not all people, not all civilisations across the universe, in fact non of them have such a diversity of emotion although they may have much love they may not have been empowered or enabled to use humour. Indeed humour has been uniquely evolved upon the earth plane because there has been so much choice given, so when the beings come to visit you they are shocked and amazed at the humour. People like Azgar, from the Siriun network, do have a similar vibration they have much love and they can tune into humour very easily and use it upon this earth plane as a form of communication.

This is not used upon their own planet because it is not necessary so you must come to realise different beings have different powers to work at different levels. But as I say with the Siriuns, they have also been in contact with this planet for many millions of years and they are delighted by the way that you may teach them. You see there is a saying 'you reap what you sow' and so, taken on a wide context, you have many skills and talents that other people, in some way, scientifically, may be in advance of you. But in other ways, they lack the finer tuning of the communication network that will involve humour. It will enclose so many different facets of love you will have a rich harvest of that upon this planet and other beings come here to share that with you, so, as you give you also receive.

It is quite a startling revelation that although cosmic beings, who are friends and bring positive influences, may appear to be more advanced technologically, capable of travelling through time and space as we know it (telepathic or physical transference in the 4th/5th dimension), they actually may lack what we take for granted. We have such an excess of love (often misused) that we can empower cosmic beings by offering or sending pure unconditional love to help with their progress or the progress of that particular planetary culture. We are cosmic beings!

The relationship of Star Systems with Individuals and Planet Earth

KERRY
How many Stars and Planets have an influence on the Earth and what are they?

AT-HLAN
That is an impossible question to answer in a way. Although you have the obvious influences from such stars as Sirius and Vega, Polaris and Aldebaran and so on, they are linked into a network, and so star systems are linked to other star systems and so on through time and space. So there is a network throughout and, if you like, an invisible network which holds the whole of the Cosmic forces in balance and in harmony, although this is disrupted momentarily this is because the disruptions need more growth and more influences of a more positive nature to be brought about in that area of cosmic network. This also happens of course in the spiritual realms, not always is there light and harmony, there are adverse influences that also you might know about, all is not light, although of course, 'like attracts like', and if you have lead a life which is a rewarding one, in which ever direction, you receive award in that direction. For so many stars influence the planet Earth, but perhaps more importantly the planet Earth influences us. There is a two way relationship and when the power of Mother Earth, the Godess or the Spirit that abides here, waxes or wanes then it will have an effect upon the relationships it has with the planets in its system, with the Solar Logos and therefore with other stars.

You see there is a direct communication between different stars such as your sun, it is not so much the size, or the brilliance of the star that is important, but the information it has to relay to the other systems. So although there is a direct relationship, because the Earth is so important, between the Earth and the other stars it is in a sense, relayed through the star which you call the sun.

PATSY
Good afternoon At-Hlan, we have a question about the seeding of the planet and would like to know more about it; who came from what part of the Universe and why?

AT-HLAN

Influences from Altair and Arcturus were given to the early tribes in Atlantis, Egypt and in the Middle-East, This is a most complex question, you will have to bear with me.. Influences from Polaris and Sirius too. I am being told from *Telemarkus as well. That is some homework for you to do! Firstly the influences in Atlantis were not single, but there were different influences there to help with the evolutionary cycle, to help with the balance of the original spiritual influence that raised mankind from beast to spirit.

*We have not yet found this particular planet or the star but no doubt it will be discussed at the right time and place.(Also see Chapter 7)

There was a co-joining of the spirit influence with the physical body, as it were, to raise their standards. This worked very well for thousands of years until there was a division. Those who should have known better started to bring about praise to a physical God. They set up Idols as it were, and there was bloodshed, a mis-use of spiritual and physical power. There was a great deal of destruction in Atlantis, for we cannot break Universal Law, we cannot take away freedom of choice. There was much destruction, but before that destruction there were people sent out to colonise other areas such as Egypt, India and on the mainland of North America. So the Light was carried by small numbers of people and from these small numbers of people the Light was spread.

There was more extra-terrestrial influence particularly in the establishment of the early dynasties in Egypt. The people saw telepathic thought projections of the people who seeded there, which is now established in their mythology where they have half beast, half man. This is a confusion of the influence of the beings that have come from different planets to seed. When we say 'seed' it is more of an addition to the genetic system.* Power is given to certain people so that they are empowered within the rules of choice to develop in certain ways to lead people to the right hand path rather than the left hand path. The seeding in and around Jedda, Mecca, Medina and Babylon was to bring tribes into harmony with each other. Again this was not to be, for at a later date there was a separation of the tribes who wished to use different rituals to bring about superiority of the particular tribe.

*For further information please see the life reading in the Appendix.

If you go back five, six, seven thousand years ago, where there are influences in the sub-continent of India then you will find that there is great wisdom risen there and passed on in terms of the Vedas and so on. Even so, that was misused when the caste system was introduced again because certain people wished to hold sway over other peoples and subjugate them. It has been a frustrating time in many ways, but in other ways there has been much growth and development in ways that could not always be forseen. We have arrived at a halfway point, perhaps more than halfway in the evolution of the races that inhabit Mother Earth, because of the different influences that still shine. Although you talk about the Christ influence there are still influences that still shine in parts of this little planet called Earth, for Peace and Harmony.

There will not be one such as Jesus who comes upon the Earth Plane again, there will be many people who are influenced for the Truth. No matter what happens there will be a powerful channel of Light brought to bear in the not too distant future that will pull many people towards a new way of thinking. A new wave length will be introduced so that those who are aware will know in their heart of hearts that this influence is the Truth. They will know because of the Harmony and Love that it brings to be shared, not to be kept but to be passed on.

LENETTE
You mentioned once that we are Star seeds, could you give us more information on this please?

AT-HLAN
I can indeed. You see, many souls who incarnate on the Earth Plane at different times will pass into the spirit world. Man will go through a series of experiences there depending upon their stage of development. It does not go in linear fashion, progression for many who have been influenced from earlier times will indeed go to the world of spirit, as you call it. Some will also return to their home planet to bring extra knowledge in their next incarnation, as it were, when they return to this planet. This process has been accelerated over the last thousand years or so. It is only now that you are beginning to feel the influence of it. This is why it is a frustration for mediums who cannot seem to recall certain people for their sitters, for they are not in spirit world, they have gone to their homes, they have gone to where sometimes they need help with the development of

those peoples upon their own planets. Some may return there to add to their store of knowledge and wisdom. This will come as a surprise to other people who call themselves spiritualists and to other people who can see no further than their noses!

There has been planetary influences here from all over the cosmos, ever since mankind became what you would call - people. Indeed, without cosmic influences, it makes sense does it not,that you could not have started a peoples here without there being influences from outside of the planet, who come to help in various ways. These influences came to help the development of the physical, mental and the soul development on different levels. Part of your mind is still linked with these peoples and it is now that so many people have the veil lifted. In their hearts they know that this is a Truth and not a myth or legend.

LENETTE
At-Hlan, could you tell us whether the Extra-Terrestrials will be playing a bigger part in our every day lives and will they be here for everyone to see?

AT-HLAN
When you are at the level of understanding to see and to communicate with such people as Azgar, who was playing with Lady Kerry-Anne's leg!!, then of course you will appreciate extra-terrestrial life and you will communicate with them quite freely, as many hundreds of thousands are doing at the moment, but you cannot cast pearls before swine as the saying goes. In other words only when you have reached the level of achievement,commitment and development, when you can appreciate this, you will visualise and sense and hear those beings otherwise there would be no point, for people would, for example, be frightened. For, as you know there are millions of souls who have been dogmatised, creedalised by certain religions who taught them to be fearful of such phenomena.

What is the point of bringing spirit forms to those people for all it would confirm to them is that their priests were correct for they have already been fed the information that when spirit forms appear it is the work of adverse influences, although we know this is not so we do not wish to reinforce their own ignorance, their own bigoted outlook. But for such people there will be forward progress in the future because the priesthood will have so many positive influences that they will have to change their whole outlook, their whole 'Raison d'etre', as indeed many are moved already. If we look at the progress that has been made already in healing, when as you know the Spiritualists, Gnostics and early Christians based many of their beliefs on the power to heal, which is true and correct, they were stigmatised by many orthodox religions who are now beginning to use the same process themselves. So, this vibration that is going on at the moment is altering, slowly but surely, the way people are addressing themselves to the problems of existence upon the Earth Plane. Have I answered your question Lady Lenette ?

LENETTE
Yes thank you At-Hlan.

PATSY
We were given the gift of freedom of choice upon this planet and I have read that we are the only planet in this universe with this gift. I was wondering how the beings on other planets evolve if they do not have the same freedom of choice that we have got?

AT-HLAN
They evolve from the work that they do, the work that they have inherited, even more primitive beings than yourselves are shaped by their environment. This is quite difficult to explain, for the environment,to a degree, will shape the person upon the earth plane. If you are surrounded by beauty and love and are cherished, you will tend to grow up to be a person who is loving and caring. So the environment on the planet shapes the purpose of the entities, the people who live for a time there. Now this is not always sufficient for their own development because it is important that no one soul grows in isolation so many have incarnated from other planetary systems when they have had something to offer and something to help to shape this environment. As you have read quite rightly, there was a time when there were 'seedings', as it was called, from other planetary systems to help shape the direction of mankind and accentuate the soul growth of the earth.

SUSAN
I am trying to find something that will link in with all of what you have been saying. Are there different Gods in different dimensions, if so how do they relate to our God?

AT-HLAN

Logically there would have to be a system of communication throughout this universe and other universes which operate simultaneously with the great mind and instantaneously, so that if you will define God as being a very high and refined spiritual entity, who has much capability and energy then you will find this, for example, in relation to your sun the solar logos, is the most direct influence upon the planetary system. So you might go to the spiritual sun and say this was the God for your planetary system. However, your planetary system is as you say 'a drop in the ocean' of the cosmos and so there would be a being who is, I do not want to say in charge of, but who has influence over a galaxy. There will be higher still a being who has influence over many galaxies and so on. By influence I do not mean that they make things happen but the information is fed back to them, is fed back to somebody who is an entity who is in a higher position and so on back to the Great Mind at the centre of all things, at all levels.

Since this channeling our home circle took a long journey to the spiritual sun and I experienced a 'meeting of minds' inasmuch as there seemd to be five or six great cosmic beings present (planetary masters) who, as part of a great network, formed links with the solar logos. At a different level, another medium 'saw' a great amphitheatre with extra-terrestrial beings from different planetary systems, holding hands seated upon galleries and in the centre of all a great light which was reflected in their faces.

AT-HLAN

It is a joy to feel and see your presence. We wish to give you more information concerning the star influences upon your planet, for it is a little more complex than you thought. You see, Altair is a prime influence and has a system very close to that of the Earth plane. It has a single sun where as many of the systems have a binary sun or second sun. The Altairians bring influences very early in the evolution of mankind, back to the time of Atlantis. There is an Altairian influence on many of you who meet in these circles. There is Antares, Aldebaran, Arcturus, Betlegeuse and of course Sirius is a strong influence also. There is a triple influence from the belt of Orion, what you would call Alnitak, Alnilam, Mintaka, come not as a triple influence, but as a single influence. The Egyptians almost based it on the triple influence, as you would say today, God the Father, God the Son, God the Holy Ghost. Castor and Pollux were a single influence and combine. There is Capella and Rigel, there is Vega where many have questioned what you would call the Lion people. Alpha Centauri is an influence which combines with your sun, as you know it is the nearest Star, that combines, as it were, as a single influence. Polaris is a strong influence which also comes in with Thuban.

I think we have covered the influences upon this planet, but I am pausing for a moment to confer with my Brothers....... These seem to have been the main influences upon your system where there are close ties, or where there have been Star Seeds. In your future circle meetings you will find that there are people who wish to communicate with you from those star influences and come closer to you.

The Friends of At-Hlan, those who have contacted me through various means will come and visit if they are able, to show you their images, to bring their voices and to have telepathic communication with you. So, you have a lot to look forward to do you not! It is important that you recognise these positive influences because as you know there are negative influences also. Not always do they mean to be negative but in their inquisitiveness they have not necessarily conformed strictly to Universal Law. So, there are battles at great mental esoteric level that still have to be fought and of course won. You have a place to play in that battle, as humble as you think you are you have many strengths and in your past lives you have fought battles before. You have come to this circle because of your Spiritual and Cosmic experiences, these paths will become clear to you in the proceeding year.

There was some confusion here about the Lion People and so we were taken on a journey to a planet called Solondari, the sixth planet from Vega, and there many members of the home circle 'met' a people who were very cat-like, slim and about seven feet tall with velvet blue-grey skin. The Lion people are from Alpha Centauri and although we have at last seen them, standing upright with great telepathic sensory communication, we have not, as yet, visited their planet. At-Hlan has a more descriptive definition of the Lion people in the previous chapter.

PATSY

Could I ask a question about the different planets you were just talking about. You were saying that some of us have influences from Altair and Antares, is it possible that in past lives we have lived on many of these planets or do we come mainly from one?

AT-HLAN

You have had past lives on several of these planetary systems. This information is being given to you at this time of new awakening. You have had incarnations on Sirius, Vega and Arcturus... That is your starter for ten!! You have brought these experiences with you to empower other people on the Earth plane. Indeed it will be interesting to go into past lives with people on a cosmic plane, not just a spiritual plane. You have the power Lady Patsy to bring the Sun, the Moon and the Stars to others, for you have strong ties with those planets. So, you have brought them to bear in your more mundane existences when you have had three incarnations with the North American Indians and South American Indians, for example, the Anazasi. You knew of the Star Systems and helped to procreate and disseminate that information to those humble people. This is just one example.

At last At-Hlan has detailed the thirteen nearest influences upon planet earth, influences that he has mentioned only in part upon previous occasions but, as with other pieces of the jigsaw, he has decided that this is the time and place to 'reveal all'. I specifically refer to 'the nearest' influences for I am sure that as we build our contacts and strengthen the communication system, we will develop links with beings who journey from even further afield. As we are allowed to experience life-forms and forces from greater distances, so we travel nearer to the mind of God.

AT-HLAN

We have great pleasure, joy and humility for although we have worked for thousands of years towards empowering other people, it is a great joy for us to know that our words have been accepted and acceptable and that there are those upon the Earth plane with great vision and understanding as you all have. Although we see here that one will leave, for reasons best known to themselves, we understand and we do know that each has to find their own pathway. Perhaps one or two will return, perhaps some leave to start their own circle. This is all part of the network. Finally, I would like to thank you from my heart, from my various planes of being, for your constancy, for your commitment, for your willingness to give up your time to share with me and my channel and those who delight in communicating with you. I hope that what we have shared together has helped you to understand who you are, who we are and the great links that we have at different levels of existence. I will come to you in your larger circle and at a later date we will come together again to progress further, to combine our strengths, to shine the Light to guide others upon the pathway towards the knowledge that there is a Great Mind who works for you all the time, who has an infinite amount of Love and understanding to share with you, who is delighted when those who commit themselves understand this and so the Great Mind and we, who serve this Light, also grow in our awareness and understanding. You are part of the Great Network and we are pleased and privileged to be in that Network. We will leave you now with our Love and our Peace in the knowledge that we have progressed as you have progressed. Goodbye for the time being, goodbye with our Love.

This was the last channeled information given for this book, which has taken us on a journey that has catalogued the various aspects of existence that effect us upon the earth plane, to the lives that may touch our lives in the cosmic plane of existence. There is a cosmic mutual support system that we may tune in to if we so wish; we give love and are loved, we give help and are helped. Our progression is inextricably linked to the progression of others from the spiritual and cosmic planes, and if we wish to play our part fully, become integrated beings, then we have the means to sit down and 'switch on' to our universal responsibilities.

As the channeling for the book has progressed, so more extra-terrestrials have sent greetings and communications from the various star systems, which leads me to believe that the next book will be entitled "The Friends of At-Hlan".

Appendix 1

AZGAR INTRODUCES HIMSELF 24th August 1992

"I love you. I bring to your circle for the first time greetings from the star system Sirius".

Q. Are you male or female?

A. We are a highly evolved species so that a form of procreation takes place through thought processes rather than the corporeal love that you use on the planet earth, which we find rather amusing. But when minds get together and create a new form in our culture it can only happen for the highest purposes. This means to say that there is a special job of work for this new creation and that creation will undertake that type of work, at that place in the cosmos, which is supposed to be influenced by this being.

Q. What job of work are you supposed to be doing with us?

A. The work that I am here to do first of all is to make it known to you that indeed you are working with spirit and with cosmic influences but in a way we are spiritual people as well because we are all formed through the love of the Spiritual Creator.

Q. What do you look like?

A. We have, as you have said, a greenish sort of texture to our bodies and, as you would see us, covered by a pinkish-white light - what you would call an aura.

This is what we bring with us from our star system, do you see, this is a reflection of our energy levels. Our covering is not like skin at all, it is more like an etheric substance because in some ways we are not as solid as you because we work at a much, much higher vibratory level.

The World of Spirit is a world that does exist and is probably more real than the Earthly world in which we live. It is in fact our real home, for our life, or lives, on this Earth plane are short - like terms at school - for the purpose of learning for our own progression, the progression of mankind, Mother Earth and last but by no means least, the progression of the Cosmos, our brothers and sisters from the Stars. So, in comparison our time spent in the Spirit world in Love and Light is long and beautiful and there we find our true home. By having links with our friends from home it enables us to walk our Earthly path with the knowledge of their love and constant support and gentle guidance, just as if we were far from home a letter or telephone call to loved ones would make life a little easier to cope with as we carry their love in our hearts. Always there is a hand outstretched to guide us over the rocks and pebbles that we would otherwise stumble on; always there is a hand outstretched to catch us should we fall; always there is the healing love to make us whole again; always there is rejoicing when we see the light and walk in it; never is there punishment or chastisement if we do not - just gentle, loving guidance to bring us back to our right path. They are our friends, our loved ones, our soul mates, our guides: we are never alone. We never have to go through any despair, grief or trauma unaided. Listen to your heart, there you will hear the voice of Spirit - the True Voice of Love and Light.

Appendix 2

PAST LIFE READING 1st November 1994.

AT-HLAN

I am At-Hlan, Warrior Priest of Atlantis. I bid you welcome here this afternoon Lady Patsy, it is a pleasure to meet with you again. I hope my channel has plenty of energy this afternoon.!

We take you back firstly to Atlantean times, as you would expect, around 200,000 B.C. when your name was Tara-Mut-Tagatha. You were a 'Keeper of the Crystal' in difficult times, Tavatli times. So, I see a pyramid in Poseidonis itself, the Great Temple of Light, and you are drawing maps, they are pathways, journeys, between this Earth, Mother Earth, and two other planetary systems. The centre of this Temple is an enormous crystal, seven feet high and very large. There is light going straight out, it is a form of communication. You can put your hands on this crystal and send out your thoughts and they will be received by those who you wish to receive the message, Alpha Centauri, Sirius, Thuban, Vega; it is a case of adjusting the vibration of the crystal by bringing in others that surround the central crystal, other crystals of a certain size and shape, so you can communicate. Also you can see what might be called today, holograms of these entities in this great place of power. Which is why there are still mysteries around that area of Bimini, there is still great power there beneath the sea. So, you are female and a ' Priestess of the Light', and it is around this time also that there have been attacks by those of the left-hand pathway, not on the Temple but the surrounding area, crystals have been taken away to other places to build other Temples far away, which your friend Richard has been involved with, an unfortunate ending in that case. But this is a safe place and not only is there a high regard for 'The Father of all Light', the Solar Logos, but there is a direct relationship, for those initiates there seem to be able to vibrate to a very high rate so as to appear invisible. There is also communication with others in the initiation, so that you can mind read telepathically at great distances and this is a time of high culture in Atlantean times. People come to this Temple for learning and for cleansing. For mental stability, to balance themselves, to balance their bodies. The light rays are used for medical purposes, to cast off that which is unsightly. There are beautiful gardens which surround this

Temple and waterways, also it is guarded by warriors. It is the centre of Atlantean civilisation. It is not used for the generation of power for lighting, for directing craft or for powering the ships, it is only used for one purpose, for connecting ourselves with the Universe. From this early incarnation you understand about the Stars, about the Sun, the Seasons, the rhythms of the Earth and when you are tuned in you become part of this rhythm. All gifts are there, you can read peoples minds, you have a past memory and a future memory for all is one in this place, with these energies.

We take you now to around 20,000 B.C. when you have met your friend Sandra. You do not work in the same place, but near that place. It is working with children. There are set up what you would call today similar to Kibbutz, where people leave their children for the day, or longer periods of time ,to be looked after, to be educated in the ways of hygiene and of the 'One Light', also of mathematics, of learning, of growing, cultivation. There is a school, a library, there are scholars here. So you spend some time with children attuning them to their lives, making them aware, guiding them to their full potential. Later there is, what you might call a segregation into those areas of learning that those pupils have shown most proficiency in. An-Ata-Kaan, is your name, it means 'Mother of Light'. So you are chosen to work with the younger elements. You have also met here your daughter, she has been here too and she has gone on to work with plants in the Great Crystal Rooms, rooms of great beauty where plants are not grown just for their colour but for their scent. Here you have several children, your husband is a strong, large person, you are large people. You read of the histories of Atlantis, of the battles won and lost, of the influences brought to bear for peace and prosperity.

Later, you see, around 11,000 BC you have moved with the House of At-Hlan, so you see you have met my channel, Rohann at these times. You have also known of the House of At-Hlan and its Lords and its Household. And so, about the time before the last submergence, there have been plans to colonise in Egypt and India and the Basque Country, also in the area of New Mexico. Some have travelled in Light Ships and some by sea, for this is now a very unsettled area. You have taken with you many of the ancient scripts; this is before your scientists have documented the earlier influences of Atlantis in what is now known as Upper Egypt. You have colonised near Edfu, and you begin to absorb the cultures that are around, and civilise the area. You have telepathic communication with animals at this time, particularly Lions, for you know of the Lion people already. You bring with you what is known latterly as the 'Eye of Horus', which is the influence of the Stars and the Revelation of the Truth, and you also bring the Crystals which form the initiation of the Golden Eye. Here also there are battles won and lost and you have helped to raise buildings and small temples. You have cleared the jungles and have built small step pyramids, not as large as later, to house the crystals for teachings. You begin to educate the primitive people here and do healing in the 'Temple of Healing'. You learn and have knowledge of how to build, architecture, to balance, to direct, to use the 'Staff of Power' in the correct manner, which you have brought with you, with others, to carve, to levitate such masses to put in the correct alignment. Nefer-Tut-Mana, is your name. It is interesting, we often have names with 3 syllables, for it passes on a tradition. Sometimes these names have become continuous or parts left out, or added on, but it is part of an historic wisdom which sounds with the name and so the name has meaning.

You have become, again in Egypt, a great builder of pyramids, as a man, Imhotep. You have helped to organise and build a large pyramid for Djoser or Zoser, as he is called, a pharaoh King. You have also planned one which you do not see in your lifetime, at Giza - Chephren. His name was 'Chephren-Tut-Tenkatha, known as Chephren. It was planned by Imhotep. So you know of the designs of the pyramids, the ceilings, of the materials used, of the rituals. Again of the influence of the Stars, of Crystal power. Inetar-Hotem-Khemet, is the full name of Imhotep, so you see how several names become one in translation. It is around 3.000 BC, a little more, although scientist say a little less. Again this is a flowering of a culture, there is trade through the rivers and the seas, although the other part of Egypt is still inhabited by what you would call primitive people. There is travel by river and sea, despite opposition. The Upper and Lower Egypt have not yet been united, although there are colonies of high cultures in many areas, at Saqqara for example.

We take you, again as a man, around 600 BC, at the time of Pythagoras. So there is an influence here of the balance in the buildings and the temples, and also the teachings, esoteric teachings borrowed from Egypt and before that time. Your name is Minocrates and you are a devout supporter of this great, powerful person who shines the Light. Again, there is conflict between the left and the right. Always difficulties, sometimes there have been burnings of the books in the libraries, even at this time of high culture in Ancient Greece, for there are many different cultures and many different influences. A great trading nation which also has been touched by the Atlantean Empire in earlier times. You yourself have been attacked and wounded, taken by surprise. You have lost the sight of an eye and you have had healing to save the sight of the other eye. You have sustained several wounds in this incarnation but have grown in wisdom and to some extent retreat to teach the higher teachings in a hidden place, moving away from the great Temple.

You have also had an incarnation at the time of the Christ. You feel ill, you are unwell, you are a woman who has internal problems with the loss of blood. You touched the hem of the robe of the Master Initiate, Jesus. Your name is Jessica Araminus. You are made well for you have touched in belief, you have known of the Light and so were given the Light. You have two children, your husband is a shepherd who works also the land. One child is a sickly girl and the other is an arrogant boy. You have taken your healing from the Master to heal your daughter and this is very efficacious and powerful healing. She has a skin disease, sores, pustules and is healed in a short time. But as the son grows he turns away, he becomes a trader in silverware, beaten copper and trinkets. He moves away from the family and all he requires is wealth. He builds a great trade but is cast down with a disease similar to the plague and has died before you can go to him near Bethsheba. But the guilt is not yours, for he did not communicate and you lost sight of him.

We take you next to the culture of the Pueblo,..... Moon Child you are called in this incarnation, with 'Rising Star' whom you have met here. It is between 700-800 AD. There has been a meeting of many peoples here from early times..Lemuria, Mu. Brown skinned people who have mingled with red - skinned people. You are a painter of pots, a designer of clothing, colourful clothing, you are very clever with your hands. You have a place in the household which is very high. You still have knowledge of the influences of the Sun and the Moon. The parchments that were written upon also have the meanings that go back perhaps a thousand years before hand. A time of prosperity. Also in this life there is passed down the meaning of the White Brotherhood which is lost in time. They are seen as the 'Ancient Mystics', they would be clothed in white, with Star designs in Gold, with white feathers to the floor. It is an interpretation of the Ancient Ones, the Cosmic Ones that you knew in Ancient Atlantis; they would be known as extra-terrestrials, this is an interpretation. You also have a daughter known as 'Moon Cloud', who you will know today as your friend Lenette. So you have crossed another path from the past to the present. You have worked with pots and also with baking, for if you alter the temperature in these places they can be used for different purposes. Rising Star is a great warrior here, also he is a protector, a guide, full of Light also, for the two do not conflict. There are great rituals in which both are involved, for strength and courage for the warrior cast, and for light and creativity for those that bring colour and feeling to the culture.

We must also take you to the Anasazi tribe that you feel so closely linked with, where you have met again many of the people from the present who came to that great culture at the time of life of its full flowering, for this is an Ancient culture that had a mixture of Atlantis and Maya. Through Atlantis we would say the Olmec and the Toltec are part of this Ancient culture which would go back to 1000 BC, but now it is about 1400 AD. 'Tiensa-Kwow-Coatl' was your name. In this culture too, you have the Ancient legend of Queztl-Coatl, 'The Feathered One', the one who arrived to bring teachings, the one that shines the Light. You will find this also in different cultures under different names. There are temples here, atop of huge earthen mounds. Great Temples that are open to the sky where you can communicate with God, the Great White Father. Where you have again the influences of the Sun, the Moon and the Stars. Also, where a fire is kept burning to show the Light, as has happened in other cultures. Where the Great Ceremony of the Four Corners of the Earth takes place. The Four Corners of the Earth are drawn together, the Four Seasons, the four influences. There is a great ceremony here, a beating of drums, a chant which focuses the four influences also of the sky, the cosmic level, the spiritual level, the Earthly, of the Earth herself. These are the four. There are many who come in beautiful feathered headdresses and beautiful costumes here. It is a ceremony of great acts of daring. There is clairvoyance because people are in what would be called a semi-coma, as the drums beat and the rhythms permeate a great area, a great gathering of peoples. There is a great Light that goes up from this place. You have participated in this ceremony also. In this incarnation your husband is killed in a battle with a neighbouring tribe and you bring up three children for a time yourself, but you remarry he who is known as 'Silver Light'. He was born when lightning strikes, so he is known as 'Silver Light', also, 'He Who Flies

High'. Many people are known as 'White Eagle', but there is another name for this entity...'Silver Light' - 'White Eagle'.

We take you now to France in the late 1500's, where you are a person who has many gifts in healing - Anne-Marie Lucteau is your name, from Rennes. You are using oils and unguents to help people with diseases and healing. You have an unfortunate incarnation in that you are tortured by the Catholic Influence at that time, and you are put under great stress and strain. It is about 1582, we will be that accurate, when you are tortured by what must be the third wave of so called, 'Religious Feeling', because there is unease and disease. So to turn the people towards the Catholic belief and away from other beliefs the priests made the people suffer by misusing themselves, by setting up courts to persecute those who did not go to Church twice, who did not give tithes, money to the priesthood. So you are involved in this religious persecution and you have been disowned by your family because of the persecution which was given to them also. The court has found you guilty of evil practices, of Satan's work, which is not the Truth, so you have suffered for the cause and have died at the hands of fools, of those who have been led astray. So you were weighted down with stones and taken to a lake and drowned. It is interesting to see, to feel, to sense that in your drowning you are not afraid, you do not feel fear and you are, if not delighted, then quite happy to die quickly, to take in great gulps of water; you have not fought it, you have had a peaceful ending for you know of the Light and the Truth. So your body is taken and you have to be buried outside the cemetery, outside the 'sanctity' of the graveyard, of the Church where there are many others who have been buried who have suffered also. You have had many more lives than these, these are important lives for you, for you would have known, in this life, one of your persecutors who was a priest, who directly persecuted you, which is why he has been brought back to you for you to help him. So, there is another link there.

We search for the next important life of yours around the 1800's, where you are of the Plains tribe of the Oglala Souix, where you have met again others that you know, you have met the Lady Hannah for example in this incarnation. You are known as 'Shining Water' in this incarnation and in this one you have a balance for you have worked with water, you have worked with water for cleansing, for adding substances to, for people to inhale when they have problems in the head and in the chest and you have worked as a Medicine Woman, a Shaman. You are a female Shaman, not all of these were male. So again you have helped to heal people and to use water to bathe them sometimes, to wash them in a particular place; there is a waterfall here and a lovely glade to cleanse them and to chant the words, to give out the words, the right vibration with the words. You have worked also with the Medicine Man, there seems to be an influence in the era of he who was called 'Red Cloud' also, whose heroic influences were spread far and wide. Again you have carried water, heated water and using it in the healing of wounds. You have used fire, also hot instruments, to cauterize wounds that are infected. You have a great village, a great Lodge, here in this place, the name 'Harpers Bend' comes to mind also, for there are White Men here too who have conquered many, who have enslaved many, who have moved this tribe who still have many battles to fight. You have worked among the wounded in the battlefields, have carried them from battles. This is the last incarnation of which we speak, so you will recognise that you have great skills and talents in this life which you are using with great ability to link with many people whom you have met, who are too numerous to mention in this reading otherwise, Lady Patsy, we would spend two sides of your tape on just one lifetime! We could go back further, for example, to Lemuria, where you were a brown skinned person for there is also a link there with Mayan, Inca. So, you have been to many places where high souls have incarnated. You have suffered in others, you have been a slave in one at the time, but they are too numerous – these are your most important lives and you must know that in this incarnation where this is a new vibration similar to the High Culture in Ancient and Ancient Egypt and for a time in the High Culture in Greece. It is returning at this time very strongly and so you and my channel and others link in to this and despite the opposition it will grow and you are playing an important part. You will be surprised what between you you will achieve in your writings, in the books of which I have referred, both Rohann and yourself, and perhaps others may become involved at a later date, to help you spell out the Truths clearly to people, to shine the Light, to show them the way. You will do this for many years because you have a distant memory of these things of which I have talked and you have a great mind. And so, between you who are tuned in to the different levels of experience, the pathways, the Spiritual and the Cosmic, this is being brought together and will be disseminated, you will be surprised, to many countries. I have time for a question Lady Patsy, that has not been answered in these readings.

PATSY

I would like to ask about Alanyd, I would like to know more about that incarnation.

AT-HLAN

Yes, this was when you had an incarnation when you were brown skinned which was in Polynesia, which was a great culture before that land disappeared beneath the sea. And so you lived in Eden, in Paradise with the animals and the trees, where there was communication and love between all. This was prior to approximately 50.000 BC, so the drawing that you have refers to that time, it looks rather Mayan I think, but it goes back to that time on that large Island, but those memories were also brought to a Mayan incarnation.....- The Ancient Land of Mu, as it was sometimes called. These animals such as the Dolphin had a telepathic rapport with people and could direct people for fishing and give information about storms and so on. That is all I have time to tell you at the moment, I hope that this information has helped you with this present incarnation and given you strength and courage.

Now I leave you with my Peace, my thanks and my Love. Goodbye for the present.

SOULMATE CRYSTAL

Throughout daylight and darkness and worlds without end
You've travelled together, you and your friend.
In one life, kin; in another life wed;
Sometimes the leader, sometimes the led,
Incarnate on other planets than Earth,
Together in death, together in birth.
It is I who will guide you once again
And help you find your cosmic friend.
Call through me, pray through me; it is my goal
To help you meet your kindred soul.